When Catholic Means Cosmic

Opening to a Big-Hearted Faith

DAVID RICHO

Paulist Press
New York / Mahwah, NJ

Front cover photo by Ricardo Zerrenner; used by permission. Back cover image (background) by Claudio Balducelli / Dreamstime.com.
Cover design by Tamian Wood
Book design by Lynn Else

Library of Congress Cataloging-in-Publication Data

Richo, David, 1940
When Catholic means cosmic : opening to a big-hearted faith / David Richo.
pages cm
ISBN 978-0-8091-4932-2 (pbk. : alk. paper) — ISBN 978-1-58768-518-7 (ebook)
1. Catholic Church—Doctrines. 2. Cosmology—Miscellanea. I. Title.
BX1753.R477 2015
282—dc23

2015007234

ISBN 978-0-8091-4932-2 (paperback)
ISBN 978-1-58768-518-7 (e-book)

Published by Paulist Press
997 Macarthur Boulevard
Mahwah, New Jersey 07430

www.paulistpress.com

Printed and bound in the
United States of America

Dedicated, as is all my life,
to the glowing hearts of Jesus and Mary
where our jubilantly evolving universe
still and always abides
in wholeness, harmony,
and unfailing friendliness—

As he passes from depth to depth in his own heart
the awakened disciple reaches the
ultimate depth of the Heart of Jesus
a pointer to the ultimate recesses of the source of being.
Then, passing beyond all, freed from all bonds,
he finally comes to the Source, where, in his eternal awakening,
he discovers what he is.

—Dom Henri Le Saux, OSB, Abhishiktananda

Contents

Preface

This book attempts to present a lively way of learning about a Catholic way to God. I attempted this project first in 2000 when I taught a class on how our Catholic faith has universal dimensions: "Catholic Means Universal," and put together notes and perspectives that became a workbook by that name to be used for similar classes. Since then, I have entered more deeply into the work of Pierre Teilhard de Chardin, Raimondo Panikkar, Karl Rahner, Hans Kung, Thomas Merton, and other theologians who contemplate faith from the evolutionary perspective. Many of us have found helpful gear for life's journey in what science and the new evolutionary theology have given us.

In this book I expand and update my original work to show how contemporary cosmology fits with and enriches our sense of Catholic teachings and spirituality. By grace, I feel much more outfitted for a lively faith. I was ordained a Catholic priest in 1966. Now I am no longer in the official ministry, but my work as a teacher, therapist, and writer feel like ministry—a realization that fills me with gratitude. I left nothing behind from my Catholic past, only annexed and integrated it into my present realizations from theology and psychology. What follows in these pages offers you the results of that felicitous and challenging enterprise.

—Santa Barbara, 2014

Introduction

Our consciousness, rising above the growing (but still too limited) circles of family, country, and race, shall finally discover that the only truly natural and real human unity is the spirit of the earth.

—Pierre Teilhard de Chardin, *Building the Earth*

When Catholic means cosmic, everything wonderfully widens. Our faith becomes a trust without limit. Our hope overflows with expectancy. Our love stretches beyond all barriers. Who we are expands. We see that we are more than ego. We live in a larger orbit, the divine life is in and around us always and everywhere.

The earth is more than a planet that we inhabit temporarily as a stopover between birth and death. We appreciate that it is central to our spiritual path: "Heaven *and earth* are full of your glory." The word *glory* in biblical terms means "numinous, divine epiphany." We see earth described by Jacob in this exquisite way: "How awesome is this place! This is none other than the house of God, and this is the gate of heaven" (Gen 28:17).

The word *cosmic*, as used in this book, means "extended without limit, totally inclusive, unconditionally welcoming." Thus, with a cosmic consciousness, *salvation* means more than "my getting to heaven." It is about the consummation of history in the infinitely extended arms of an all-embracing Christ. Indeed, St. Cyril of Jerusalem wrote of Christ: "He stretched out His hands on the Cross, that He might embrace the ends of the world."[1] We see this same image in the Christ of the Andes—arms outstretched to present us with a new cosmic crucifix.

Our sense of our calling widens: The word *catholic* means "universal," so it calls us to a caring connection with all people. The word *cosmic* means "universe-wide," so it takes us a further step: we open to a sense of relationship with all that is.

The source of all this widening is the Holy Spirit. Here are five visits of the Spirit that illustrate the cosmic colors in the good news about our life in God:

The Bible begins this way: "In the beginning when God created the heavens and the earth, the earth was a formless void and darkness covered the face of the deep, while a wind from God swept over the face of the waters. Then God said, 'Let there be light'; and there was light" (Gen 1:1–3).

The Gospel story begins with the coming of the Holy Spirit upon Mary: "The Holy Spirit will come on you, and the power of the Most High will overshadow you; therefore the child to be born will be holy; he will be called the Son of God" (Luke 1:35).

The ministry of Christ begins with an animating by and mandate from the Spirit: "The Spirit of the Lord is upon me, because he has anointed me to bring good news to the poor" (Luke 4:18a).

The Church is born from the coming of the Spirit upon Mary and the apostles: "When the day of Pentecost had come, they were all together in one place....All of them were filled with the Holy Spirit" (Acts 2:1, 4).

In the final book of the Bible, we are all given something to hope for and expect: "The Spirit and the bride say, 'Come.' And let everyone who hears say, 'Come.' And let everyone who is thirsty come. Let anyone who wishes take the water of life as a gift" (Rev 22:17).

A cosmic religion is one that opens us to these five gifts so they can come through as callings to each of us:

The first visit of the Holy Spirit is creation in which all that is becomes holy. We are called to honor the holiness of the universe as the body of God.

The second visit is the incarnation. We are called to join in the ongoing incarnation of an evolving cosmos by letting Christ be born in us each day.

The third visit of the Holy Spirit is spreading the good news far and wide. We are called to co-create a world of justice, peace, and love, the purpose of and longing in the heart of Christ.

The fourth visit is the birth of the believing community. We are called to be the Church in the world so that it is not parochial but opens its embrace to include all people of good will.

The fifth visit of the Spirit is apocalyptic. It is the promise of a happy conclusion to our human story, a consummation of history in universal salvation. We read in Acts: "Heaven must receive him until the time comes for God to restore everything, as he promised long ago through his holy prophets" (3:21 NIV). In this vision, God is the spouse who showers us with mercy upon mercy. Our calling is to live in such a way as to usher in a new heaven and a new earth. It is blessed by Father, Son, and Spirit—God as a community of love in whose image we are made.

St. Athanasius says, "God became human so that humans could become God."[2] We are part of the mystery of God because we are made in the image of Christ. He is the Word made flesh and we are unique syllables of that Word. Christ is the supreme revelation of the God who is love. In this way, he shows us the ultimate goal and purpose of evolution: to raise consciousness to a level of love and wisdom that extends throughout the world.

We usually limit our view of the incarnation to the moment in the annunciation at which Mary became pregnant with Christ, when God became man. The cosmic Christ expands the scope of the incarnation. The incarnation begins at the Big Bang. In that incarnation, the Divine enters matter. At the annunciation, the Divine enters humanity. At Pentecost, the Holy Spirit incarnates the Church. At every human birth, God becomes incarnate in an individual called to a cosmic purpose. All these are one experience of epiphany in a variety of manifestations. All are incarnations happening now, not only in history. Thus, we appreciate the bigness of our faith when we see how the incarnation manifests over and over. It is too deeply a part of our life with God to be limited to once.

Religious concepts are code words for the most mysterious and profound possibilities of our humanity. What we applied only to God comes to be seen as a calling from God to show that we really are made in his image.

A new look at religion—what we do in this book—is a glimpse into the vast cosmos and its evolutionary impulse. We see into the lifetime of the universe. In our family album we see into our own lifetime. The images remain in our memory throughout our lives. This happens because they tell the story of us and those we love. Religious images also remain in us for a lifetime. They reflect the archetypal, commonly held memories of the whole human family. They tune into truths inherited from our ancestors that now still live in our psyches. Such images carry deep and mysterious meanings yet to be revealed, never to be fathomed. This may be why they do not go away. They are waiting for us to enter and touch them. Our family album shows us growing physically. The universal symbols of humanity show us who we are as spiritually evolving beings. They are cosmic in scope.

Our Catholic heritage was often tied to the classical Greek philosophical tradition. It emphasized the omnipotence of logic and reason over intuition and vision. Our exposure to our religion was almost entirely synonymous with exploring the philosophy of Plato and Aristotle. This was helpful but led to a diminishing of room for the mystical, the intuitive, the miraculous, the archetypal, all the avenues that connect us to the transcendent and reveal the vibrant spirituality we seek so fervently today.

This book proposes a liberated, that is, a fearless, far-reaching, and open Catholicism. We seek a bigger view than the one we first saw: We want the religious instinct of reverence rather than the fear of hell. We want religious images that mirror the depths of our souls rather than ones we see far above our reach. We want religious rituals that enact initiation into the company of Jesus rather than institutionalism. In all this, we see no division between religion and spirituality; they correlate to and supplement one another. That happens when faith is not limited to creeds but opens into active, caring love for all beings.

By faith, we become here-and-now embodiments of God's love. We manifest the Creator of love, the Redeemer of love, and the Sustainer of love. True faith in the gospel of Jesus is summarized in Matthew 25:31–46, where we read that the kingdom is for those who feed the hungry, shelter the homeless, clothe the naked, and visit the sick and imprisoned. Faith is shown first of all in having and showing love for everyone. This is our first step into the bigness of our faith since it shows it to be about universal love, not only for humans but for the whole planet. In this way, faith is a driving force in our ongoing evolution as cosmically connected beings.

This book is not iconoclastic. Rather, it respects icons. After all, they are accurate and comforting mirrors of the depth of our human and divine interior life, as we noted above. They were never meant to be up and beyond us. They were designed in and by the spiritually alive psyche to be the looking glasses for us to pass through and thereby let the light through. Every picture and statue we lit candles for held the secret of the One in all of us. They were and are mirrors of our true nature.

Our true nature beyond ego is a grace, God's life in ours. Our deepest identity is nothing less than a universal interconnectedness indissolubly in union with the Divine. Thomas Keating shows us the mystical depth of this realization:

"Our basic core of goodness is our true self....The acceptance of our basic goodness is a quantum leap in our spiritual journey. God and our true self are not separate. Though we are not God, God and our true self are the same thing."[3] This is the challenge of a Catholic faith that is cosmic; it includes all that is God and who we are.

Religion is often rejected nowadays because of its dualism—we down here, God up there, and no room for nature. I am suggesting that the dualism is a distortion that can be corrected when we perceive a new triune ratio: the human is to the Divine as to the natural. All three are one: a depth psychologist can be a naturalist can be a theologian. This is not new in Catholicism. It has an ancient lineage going back to mystics like Meister Eckhart and linking to modern contributors like Pierre Teilhard de Chardin and Thomas Merton. St. Francis expressed the connection between God, nature, and all of us in his poem, "Brother Sun, Sister Moon...." Thus, we are not innovators but inheritors. There were always people who thought in big ways. For instance, we see cosmic consciousness reflected in the ancient Greek Orphic ritual of pre-Christian times. The soul is instructed about the journey after death: "You will be asked: 'Who are you? Where are you from?' Do not give your human name. The deceased answer: 'I am [a child] of the Earth and starry sky.'"[4] We are reminded of the familiar words of Carl Sagan: "There is not one cell in your body that was not once part of a star."

For those who have been away from the Church for a while, our faith may sometimes seem like a broken cathedral after a bombing: here half a God, there half a Virgin. Beliefs can remain in us from childhood with no logical unity, based more on what had consoled us than on internal continuity or conscious choice. However, it is never too late to find in the contradictory and seemingly ill-fitting pieces something sufficient to begin rebuilding. This is as legitimate as reconstructing a cathedral from its own ruins. We cannot live permanently in these ruins, but we can begin again in them. The part of the cathedral that was made of wood has burned away. The part that was made of stone has remained. Our faith-cathedral may look strange, as a single charred chimney looks strange after a fire has burned away a house. The challenge is to visit the ruins, to sit in the midst of them, to be fair witnesses of the wreckage. Then from the ashes we awaken to what has never nor can ever die: faith, hope, and love—now cosmic in their stunning expanse. A new Catholicism is stubbornly insisting on being born today, every day. We can be its midwives. What follows in the proceeding chapters gives us some skills—and encouragement too.

The true abyss is the human soul....The terrifying immensity of the heavens is an external reflection of our own immensity.... In the sublime inner astronomy of the heart...we see the Milky Way in our own souls.

—Léon Bloy, *Le Mendiant Ingrat*,
translated by Jorge Luis Borges in *Labyrinths*

CHAPTER ONE

The Bigness of Our Faith

Christ's life is not simply a model for how to live, but the living truth of my own existence. Christ is not alive now because he rose from the dead two thousand years ago. He rose from the dead two thousand years ago because he is alive right now.

—Christian Wiman, *My Bright Abyss*

Cosmology is the branch of philosophy or astronomy dealing with the origin and structure of the universe. In the old traditional cosmology, we found ourselves in a triple-decker universe, three-tiered: heaven above us, earth under us, and hell below us. (Purgatory was the mezzanine, pictured as between earth and heaven.)

This traditional view relies on ranking. Heaven holds the highest rank; earth has middle rank; hell has the lowest rank. This is a naïve imitation of the ranking we see in an organization or a family. Ranking in the military refers to different levels of skill, authority, and duties. Ranking in any system fosters order, safety, security, and survival for the group. So we can see how it has value. In a more open form of classification, however, rank yields to levels among equals. Thus, we acknowledge the unique gifts each person brings to the table. Then we do not think of rank as one-up, one-down, only diverse orders of service and responsibility.

The old cosmology legitimates a top-down hierarchy. The new cosmology is a holarchy: each part is equally important to the whole. This style applied to an institution is more likely to result in a hierarchy of service rather than of control. Mystics knew this to be the way the world works, all of us one with the God within, Christ consciousness, indwelling Spirit.

In the old cosmology, not only the triple-decker universe has rankings, but each of the three floors does too, in ways that now seem quaint.

Heaven is divided into three ranks: God, angels, saints. In God, the three persons—Father, Son, Holy Spirit—are equal, no ranking.

Among the angels there are nine ranks, divided into three spheres: The first sphere contains the contemplative angels, continuously adoring God: the Seraphim, Cherubim, and Thrones. The second sphere is concerned with creation; they order the universe: the Dominations, Virtues, and Powers. The third sphere is comprised of messengers from heaven to earth: Principalities, Archangels, and Angels (including guardian angels).

Likewise, the saints in heaven are ranked in honor: Mary is supreme, followed by St. Joseph. They are followed by the apostles, the canonized saints, and finally all holy people now in heaven.

The *earth* realm is ranked in accord with levels of consciousness: people, animals, plants, and minerals.

There are also rankings in *hell*: Lucifer or Satan, a fallen Seraph, is the prime demon. His fellow rebel angels rank below him. Likewise the damned are divided in accord with the seriousness of their evil deeds, for example, Judas or Hitler are pictured as suffering more than less egregious sinners.

This old view, familiar from our childhood, is tied to a spatial analogy. It is far too limited to be the organizing principle of our theology or spirituality. Our challenge now is to loosen our grip on the old paradigm. The new cosmology emphasizes unitive consciousness, one that moves away from strictures and structures of control, hierarchy, dualism, division, and ranking. Instead we see the universe as one ever-evolving cooperative web of life. It works by interactive love and its order is not based on control but on respect for the diverse gifts of humans and nature.

In cosmic faith, the universe is nothing less than the Mystical Body of God. The Sacred Heart of Jesus is the heart of this Body. The Holy Spirit is the soul.

Now "the kingdom is within you" rings a liberating bell in us. The new cosmology releases us from the trance of spatial metaphors and dualism: we are all one universe evolving, unfolding, and enfolding. Heaven and hell are states of consciousness within the whole, ways of being, not places we are in. We construct, moment by moment, states of heaven, hell, or purgatory. In this view, ranking is about generosity, not prestige. The Church is not listed top to bottom as pope, bishops, priests, deacons, and finally laity. It is a round table of co-contributors to an ongoing planetary Pentecost. At this table we hear Jesus calling us to co-create a world of justice, peace, and love. We can't help noticing—and appreciating—the bigness of this cosmic view and its cosmic calling.

THE COSMIC CHRIST

A dynamic universe provokes the idea and the understanding of a dynamic God....This is a God who is deeply immersed in a love affair with the beloved, the creation which flows out of his divine heart....To live in the risen Christ is to see the world with new eyes...to live from a new center of love....What happens in Jesus is to continue in our lives as well, if the Christ is the fullness of what our lives are intended to be.

—Ilia Delio, Leadership Conference of Women Religious, 2013

The term *Cosmic Christ* refers to three realizations about Christ and his role in our lives:

1. The entire cosmos was created in and through Christ: "All things came into being through him" (John 1:3).
2. The incarnation is not limited to his historical mortal body, but includes the whole universe; a unity of matter and Spirit: "The fullness of him who fills all in all" (Eph 1:23).
3. Christ came to earth out of love for us and to express his love through us—a wider purpose than the sin/ransom focus: "As the Father has loved me, so I have loved you; abide in my love" (John 15:9)

We can expand on each of these three perspectives.

1. Christ's Role in Creation

Christ is indeed not only in and for us but in and for all creation. We see the cosmic Christ in his role in creation presented explicitly in Colossians: "He is the image of the invisible God, the firstborn of all creation; for in him all things in heaven and on earth were created, things visible and invisible, whether thrones or dominions or rulers or powers—all things have been created through him and for him. He himself is before all things, and in him all things hold together" (1:15–17). Likewise, in the Epistle to the Hebrews, we see Christ's cosmic role because "he is the reflection of God's glory and the exact imprint of God's very being, and he sustains all things by his powerful word" (1:3).

To be made in the image of the God who is love means we were created to love as God does, without limit or condition. Indeed, love is the purpose of all creation. This is why Christ is the exemplar of the human story. He shows us what we are, loving incarnations of the Divine. We are a suitable venue of divine life as is our story. Each of our lives is the story of how much of God's love can happen in our lifetime and be then shown to the rest of the world. This is why we were given a lifetime—for cosmic purposes, nothing less.

2. The Cosmic Incarnation

The cosmic Christ is bigger than the Jesus who saves me. He saves me along with all that is. Hence, he is a cosmic redeemer. We see the cosmic extent of Christ's kingdom in Philippians: "So that at the name of Jesus every knee should bend, in heaven and on earth and under the earth" (2:10). This is the embodiment of the Divine in spirit and matter. All that is has been permeated without reserve with the presence of God from the Big Bang until now. So all that *is* is holy, already, and always; all afters, all befores.

Karl Rahner points out that the cosmos is being completed in Christ and that the arc of evolution is from matter to spirit. We might say that spirit is how nature transcends itself and matter is how spirit completes itself. In humans, matter becomes conscious of itself. Consciousness is more than awareness. It is alertness and responsiveness to the power of the Holy Spirit at work in the cosmos. We then honor that work and become part of it. When we humans commit ourselves to a life of love, we align ourselves to the Holy Spirit. This is how we move toward the Divine, the fulfillment of our humanity. It is a big purpose, far more than just finding out how each of us can get to heaven.

3. Why Christ Came

St. Augustine in the fourth century, St. Anselm in the eleventh century, and St. Thomas in the thirteenth century presented the incarnation as happening mainly in response to our sins. Benedictine theologian Rupert of Deutz, in the eleventh century, proposed that the incarnation is too great an event to be only about making up for sin; it would have happened anyway because of God's love for us. This wonderfully expansive idea is also found in St. Albert the Great, Alex of Hales, St. Bonaventure, Duns Scotus, and others. A God who wants to communicate with us would not have stopped at creation to do so. The incarnation shows what God wants, an ever more intimate closeness to us. Each human birth is yet another opportunity for that wonderful possibility. This is how we are honoring God's plan. The love in God was so diffusive and gigantic, it spread itself out and became a cosmos, and it is still spreading into our expanding universe by evolution.

Fidelity to the cosmic Christ means the evolution of a cosmic consciousness in each of us. We are not here to save only ourselves, but to save the entire world. We are not here waiting for heaven, but trying to make this world the heaven it was meant to be. We are cosmic Christians when our calling is to care deeply about the planet and its endangered ecology. We are likewise moved to take action to reverse the trend of destruction of natural resources. We are also here to end war, prejudice, torture, genocide, and all the dark enterprises of evil. A cosmic Christ is not just a bigger image for us to bask in. It is a challenge to live heroically because we see salvation as deeply related to ecological, political, and cultural change.

The cosmic Christ is not separate from the Trinity. St. Bonaventure contemplated the Trinity in terms something like this: The Father is love as the source of goodness and expresses his love in the Word, Christ. The Word manifests divine love interiorly and when that love becomes exteriorized it becomes the creation of the cosmos with Christ as its exemplar. The love between Father and Son is the Holy Spirit, love active in the world from the beginning and active now in all of us and in all that is.

Thus, every cell, every molecule, and every heart is a direct manifestation of divine love. The entire cosmos is how God shows the vastness of divine love ever outpouring itself into all that is. Every being, without exception, is therefore a unique articulation of divine love, something sacred with a sacred calling to spread the love we came from and are. There is one web of life from one love and all life is loved by and is the love of the God who is love.

Cosmogenesis is a word that refers to the origin and evolution of the universe. Since it is evolutionary, the world is still becoming itself. Thus, God's creation is not a single discrete event. In a cosmic, that is, unlimited, perspective, we can say that since love from God is shown in matter and still goes on, creation is still happening.

By the third century, creation *ex nihilo*, that is, out of nothing, was the theological view that prevailed. However, the mystics saw creation as happening *ex profundis*, that is, out of the profound depths of divine life. The notion of an overhead, omnipotent, interventionist God who creates all by fiat, from nothing, is limited because it is dualistic. The creative, dynamic, immanent Spirit of the cosmos, still creating and incarnating in us out of the depths of divine reality, invites our co-creative participation.

Pierre Teilhard de Chardin used the word *Christogenesis* to refer to the origin and goal of creation: the cosmos as Christ's Body. God created the world in the image and likeness of Christ, another way of referring to the unity of Spirit and matter, as we see in the incarnation. Evolution is the process by which that purpose is fulfilled: the world becomes his kingdom of justice, peace, and love. That is what is meant by God being "all in all" (1 Cor 15:28). Thus, cosmogenesis and Christogenesis are one and the same. This is the cosmic view further stated in the Epistle to the Colossians: "You have come to fullness in him" (Col 2:10). "There is no longer Greek and Jew, circumcised and uncircumcised, barbarian, Scythian, slave and free; but Christ is all and in all" (Col 3:11).

The Incarnation thus personalizes evolution because Christ is more than the historical Jesus, but is the center of a spiritually oriented evolution: "For in him the whole fullness of deity dwells bodily" (Col 2:9). Incarnation shows the purpose of the world, why it was made. Thus, the unfolding, evolving, of the universe is the unfolding of Christ's identity and ours: "Mystery hidden for ages in God who created all things" (Eph 3:9). The urgency in evolution is for transcendence, going beyond what we are now to what we can be. Our drive to evolve is the same energy by which the whole world evolves. The whole universe is on a spiritual path. A religion is cosmic when it opens to this possibility and is designed to help it happen here and now. Judy Cannato wrote, "Evolution of creation proceeds through... active self-transcendence—the presence of the Holy Spirit, within each creature pressuring it to evolve."[1]

This call to evolve shows the bigness of our destiny. The religious images in our childhood were consoling but did not often show the cosmic extent of our faith. Pierre Teilhard de Chardin, in *The Mass on the World,* relates an experience of finding the cosmic in a familiar image of the Sacred Heart:

> Your main purpose in this revealing to us of your heart was to enable our love to escape from the constrictions of the too narrow, too precise, too limited image of you which we had fashioned for ourselves. What I discern in your breast is simply a furnace of fire; and the more I fix my gaze on its ardency the more it seems to me that all around it the contours of your body melt away and become enlarged beyond all measure, till the only features I can distinguish in you are those of the face of a world which has burst into flame.

This mystical comment immediately shows us an example of what is meant by a bigness of faith. The familiar image of Jesus showing his heart on the outside depicts him dressed in red and white garments. He has a beard, long hair, and is looking at us. Pierre Teilhard de Chardin sees the physical aspects fade away and the Sacred Heart is at the center of the entire cosmos. It is the center of the universe. We see more than a person with a heart; we see the heart of the cosmos in Christ.

In the past, the Sacred Heart of Jesus was also associated with promises about our personal salvation. Pierre Teilhard de Chardin brings the focus of devotion to the larger world. He sees the heart of Christ as burning with caring love for the needs of all humankind, not only the individual honoring his picture. In this context, our religion is about the needs of the planet. Every belief in our religion has bigness once we let go of the individualistic perspectives we were brought up with. Then we begin to see the vast evolutionary dimensions on which our cosmic faith is built.

Finally, we can summarize and expand on all we are seeing in this section. Jesus makes God someone to touch, someone to talk to, someone to love, someone who makes us feel loved: "I have loved you with an everlasting love; therefore I have continued my faithfulness to you" (Jer 31:3). The incarnation shows us the full extent of these words of Jeremiah. Jesus shows us the God who is love, loving us and all the cosmos.

Now the natural and supernatural are no longer opposites but correlates. Divine and human, spirit and matter come together in Christ, are what Christ is, and are what we are. The incarnation shows us the fullness of our identity. The life of Jesus is thus not simply his story but ours. He is the anointed one and so are all of us, anointed to bring good news to the world, to bless it, to save it. When Jesus says, "Come, follow me," this is what he means. In his public life, he never asked for adoration, only imitation.

At the resurrection, Jesus, the historical person, became Christ. This shows us our destiny, to die to ego and embrace our full spiritual identity. We are called to move from ego into a new way of being alive. Christ showed that new way to us in his risen life. Now our purpose is not self-centered but cosmos-centered. Jesus showed us where his tabernacle is, the universe. That is where he was looking when he said, "This is my Body."

> *Christ has a cosmic body that extends throughout the universe.* —Pierre Teilhard de Chardin

OUR LARGER LIFE

> *I hear two voices in my head: the ego, which is the voice of fear, and the Holy Spirit, which is the voice of love....The good news is that the Holy Spirit can make use of anything, even ego.* —Brother Tikhon

In early history, humans had very little sense of a personal identity, only of a collective identity. Each individual was a part of the whole tribe or city-state. With Plato, we see a sense of an individual personality. This seed came to fruition centuries later in the Enlightenment.

The birth of psychology is another high point in our growing consciousness of an individual self, its coherence, its fragility, its vulnerability to childhood upbringing, its defenses, its gifts, and its self-healing powers. In modern psychology there is no separate, unchanging self.

The evolution of religious consciousness reflects humanity's growing realization about its true identity. It is more than physical and psychological; it is spiritual. Spirituality is transcendence of ego and connectedness with all beings. We are individual identities connected to one another and to the cosmos. This connectedness in which we all abide is what Carl Jung called the Self, the aliveness in us that is bigger than our ego, the same aliveness that is in nature and in God. Our true Self is a deep oneness with all that is—what the Sufis call our "Supreme Identity." Thus, our sense of the cosmic begins with ourselves. Alan Watts wrote, "Every one of us is an aperture through which the whole cosmos looks out."[2]

We are thus more than an ego, body, and personality. We are a unique articulation of the cosmos and we are given a lifetime to find ourselves in it. In this book, we look for our religion in it too. We find it because the cosmic Christ is the Christ in us. Indeed, the traditional teaching is that all was created in the likeness of Christ: "All things came into being through him" (John 1:3) *A cosmic Christ means a cosmic all of us.* A cosmic sense of our faith means that our life is the life of Christ and so is everything else.

We are persons with unique ego qualities, but the inner depth of us is one and the same, hence cosmic. That is what mystics called the God within, not a separate person, but the Source of all personhood and all of nature too. God is personal in the sense that personal denotes conscious, not in the sense of separate and distinct as individual humans are. Thus, for mystics, though God is not someone else, God relates to us, and we to God; mutually connected and communing. Protestant theologian Paul Tillich wrote, "God is not a person but not less than personal."[3] The God/Source is unconditional, that is, beyond conditions or one-sided attributes.

The pagan mystic Plotinus made this same point when he distinguished the God who is the higher Self from the ground of being that he called "the One without characteristics." He used a metaphor to express his mystical experience of fusion with the One: "The flight of the alone to the Alone." He added that mystical union was like having light so flood our vision that all things become illuminated, but all we really see is the light that is illuminating them. In all our inner life and in the entire universe, we see only the Godhead, the light on, in, and behind appearances. Life exists within, between, and around us. The core of that life is God. This is how God is everywhere and "everywhen" and everyone, nothing less than the mystical body/soul of the cosmos. Carl Jung called the Self archetype "God within." God in Catholic belief is triune: God within, Christ consciousness, and indwelling Spirit.[4]

Neither a thinking "I" nor an ego can ever be large enough to encompass all that we are. A larger life than that of ego animates us. It is the true or higher Self that participates in the life of the Divine, the "higher power" than that of ego. Through grace, the Holy Spirit enables us to use our ego as an instrument of justice, peace, and love. This is what Carl Jung called the ego/Self axis, the goal of human individuation.

We read in 1 Timothy 2:4, "[God] desires everyone to be saved and to come to the knowledge of the truth." In other words, that which is deepest in us wants our wholeness to happen. This is the same point that Emma Jung, in *The Holy Grail*, makes psycho-spiritually: "An inner wholeness presses its still unfulfilled claims upon us." There seems to be an irrepressible capacity, ever alive in human nature, to transcend itself. This yearning in us shows itself in every wish to make good things last, in every attachment to what fascinates us, and in every search for something to hold onto. These are spiritual longings since they are aimed at that which endures beyond, that is, transcends, the limiting exigencies of time. Carl Jung says that our yearning for the spiritual is as strong in us as the desire for sex.

Faith originates in our capacity for transcendence, finding our larger life beyond our ego. The word *transcendence* applied spiritually therefore refers to that in us that lives beyond the limitations of ordinary consciousness. Evolution is transcendence because it involves a continual process of going beyond old forms in favor of new ones. This does not mean that the transcendent has to be outside us. A higher power than ego can also be within us, that is, a vibrant and intuitively tuned inner life. This can be what is traditionally referred to as the immanence of God, the indwelling of the Holy Spirit: *I am more than I seem to be and something more than me upholds me.*

Once one acknowledges the reality of a transcendent "higher power," there is no distinction between merely natural and totally supernatural. Everything is, as Karl Rahner concludes, "supernatural existential." Implicit in concrete reality is the transcendent, something enduring behind fragile—yet translucent—appearances. "The mode of God's immanence is transcendence," says Gregory Baum, who speaks of faith as "depth experience," how we consolidate meanings and render our mortal story and our transcendent destiny one coherent continuity. In this context, evolution is itself an urge toward transcendence, a divine force in us and all things toward transcendence, that is, toward God. Grace is what makes it possible for us to say yes to this inner impulse. This is what is meant by the shift from the outsider God to the insider God. It was not discovered in modern times but was rather rediscovered, since there were always sages, mystics (and heretics), who grasped this truth. In the frightened and limited view of humans as merely rational animals, an elevation to divine life is required for wholeness. In the more open and trusting view, just being and acting in human ways is enough, since human includes heart and that heart is God-as-love.

We now can appreciate that everything is larger than it

appears. God/the Self transcends ego; love transcends ego. There is no dualism, only an invisible realm within all visible things. The entire cosmos is the indwelling Holy Spirit. The early Christian theologian Origen preached, "Understand that you are a little world and that the sun, moon, and stars are within you."[5] In this view we no longer seek to dominate nature but to serve and preserve it. We are not on the earth but are involved intimately in this stunning phase of its evolution—a cosmic spiritual purpose indeed.

Human nature and divine nature are two sides of a single coin. God present in us means that there is something in us that dares us to transcend ego with all its arrogant boasts and its fretful limitations. Peter Berger, a Lutheran sociologist, speaks of five "signals of transcendence."[6] These signals help us believe in the transcendent. He lists:

- Our innate longing to find order in chaos
- Our playfulness
- Our indomitable hope
- Our outrage at evil
- Our irrepressible sense of humor

We can add the following:

- Our ability to go on loving no matter how we are treated by others
- The durability of our capacity to love no matter what happened to us in the past
- Our willingness to put ourselves second, even to risk our lives for others
- Our capacity to forgive and let go, not to give up on people

- Our ineradicable belief that there is goodness and the possibility of redemption in every human heart
- Our sense of accompaniment by a protecting presence
- Our knack for showing our best when things are at their worst
- Our intuition that reveals more than we logically know
- Our refusal to accept defeat in the face of unalterable odds
- Our discontent with what lies within our grasp and our consequent striving for what lies beyond our grasp (our inclination to stretch)
- Our power to say, do, or be something that leads to healing ourselves and others
- Our abiding sense that the universe is friendly and that there is a loving intent in all that happens to us

In short, we have it in us to put love before survival, as the nursing infant smiling at his mother demonstrates when he thereby loses the nipple. We also have it in us to go beyond appearances. This is a way of saying that we have a transpersonal identity beyond our personal one: "Your names are written in heaven" (Luke 10:20).

Something in us keeps defying the facts at hand. We are more than the facts show or that our minds can know. We leap beyond limits, sometimes even beyond the conditions of human existence. As Karl Rahner says, "We taste fullness in the void, dawn in gloom, discovery in renunciation."[7] We are more than we seem, bigger than we look in a photograph. The reality behind our and all appearances is the Divine. We both see it and participate in it. "A rose is a rose is a rose" also means "a rose is more of a rose than I ever realized as I am more of a Self than I imagined."

The Renaissance in art began with a realization that the essence of human existence is divinity. Our renaissance of faith happens when the transcendent breaks through our quotidian reality and we begin to trust that it is both in us and is everywhere upholding us. The breakthrough, the experience, and the risk of trust in the midst of uncertainty are all the ways the personal ego enters an axis of power with the transpersonal Self. Wholeness is arrival at that axis. Joy is what it feels like since we are at last fulfilled. This is how individuation, integration of our local daily ego life and the divine life, most fruitfully happens.

The vastness of the psyche is exactly congruent to the vastness of the universe. Psyche reflects cosmos. Our joy is to experience something transcendent in nature and to say, "This is familiar; I feel this in the depths of myself." The meaning out there matches the indwelling Spirit. We see this realization in St. Bonaventure: "The gifts of the Holy Spirit are in all things."[8] We realize that the sacred is not an object but a continually unfolding reality that reflects itself in us and in the entire cosmos.

Meister Eckhart rewrote St. Paul's words: "Nothing can separate me from the love of God" as "Nothing can separate me from what I find within me." He adds, "In my breakthrough I see that God and I are one." God is, in this mystical view, the actualization of our love, wisdom, and healing powers.

Likewise, access to God does not require the mediation of patriarchal authority. Bruno Borchert says that this mystical tradition is universal and, though it may differ externally, "in essence everywhere it is everywhere the same: it is the experimental knowledge that, in one way or another, everything is interconnected, that all things have a single source."[9] This is a mystical intuition of connection and communion: people and nature, people and people, people and God. What more can cosmic mean? This is what our faith looks like when it has cosmic dimensions:

- God is too big to be someone.
- There is no duality, no "out there."
- Our deepest reality is God within, Christ consciousness, indwelling Spirit.
- Reality, in the sense of what happens to us, is how God is present in our lives, what is meant by "the will of God" to which we say, "Yes, thy will be done."
- We are jubilant about our awareness of the cosmos as one mystical body.
- We are free from the delusional sense of a separate self with all its "me first" attitudes and its misuse of people and the environment.
- We have a sense that the energy that started and maintains existence is the same energy that started and is maintaining us.
- "We were made in the image of God" does not mean God having eyes and ears but having the same flow and energy of universal love we can all participate in.
- We have found out that there is a love in us stronger than any fear.
- Our way of praying shows that God is too near to be addressed as separate. Prayer is not a letter sent to someone out there, but recognition of divine presence in any here and now, no matter how unwelcome.

- We gain an evolutionary consciousness: an unflappable sense of connection to the web of life.
- We are impelled by a passion to express and contribute our unique gift to the benefit of all beings.
- Our sense of divine judgment is not about reward and penalty, but about infinite mercy.
- What we seek is yearning to be found inside us.
- We trust that many graces are trying to come and we widen our narrow entryway to welcome them.

Finally, when we say there is a larger life in us, a life of the cosmic Christ, what are we basing that on? There is no proof. Yet, we can trust an inner evidence that cannot be contradicted and does not require substantiation. This is what is meant by "mystical intuition."

Here is a distinction that might help us understand this: We recall the statement, "I believe it because the Bible tells me so." This is faith based on the authority of revelation. Compare it to this affirmation: "We have seen his glory" (John 1:14). This is faith based on personal experience of a larger life in Christ.

Here is an example of the difference between the two ways of believing: Medical sources say that a daily aspirin regimen is useful for heart health. We believe this based on authority. Dietitions say that beginning the day with oatmeal is better than beginning it with a doughnut. We believe this because we tried it and liked how we felt after. In addition, the first statement about the aspirin is information. But the second statement about oatmeal *rings true inside us.* It feels right whether or not we try it. We believe in the value of the oatmeal breakfast not because of any authoritative voice but because of how it settles in us as true, the right thing to do.

The perennial philosophy, depth psychology, mystical realizations, and scriptures in all traditions are unanimous. They all aver that there is a larger life in us than ego, that all that exists participates in it, that the Divine is in all things, that we live in a world of oneness not separateness, and that we have a destiny beyond our personal goals. Our belief in these cannot be based on the word of authorities. To be real for us, it has to ring true in our deepest being. It does not come to us but feels as though it was always in us. We then feel it is true, experience it that way, and live our lives from it. The bigness of faith is the courage to accept the felt truth that perches in us and yet keeps arising from deep within us: "Mine eyes have seen the glory."

A NATURALLY RELIGIOUS INSTINCT

An ineradicable and core yearning in the psyche responds to religion. This is because religion has preserved, in its unique vocabulary, rituals, and enduring beliefs, the spiritual wisdom of the ages. The themes endure throughout the centuries since they reflect an inner truth we both possess and are not ready to know fully. This is because the tool we use, our thinking mind, is too limited for the hugeness of the truth involved. Faith does not make the impossible possible, but reveals what was always the reality. Faith makes the unthinkable real, the impossible ordinary.

In the depths of the psyche, sacred meanings are revealed. The innermost core of ourselves is a Sinai, a locus of revelation. Eventually, we find an indestructible diamond revelation about us and the cosmos, the spiritual meaning that has survived the decades of our life and the millennia of the world's life.

Religion survives for the same reason that anything

survives, because it serves a function, as Darwin would say. Religion is the limited ego's response to limitlessness. It thus recommends reverence toward powers beyond its control. A religious attitude toward our inner life is a reverence for ourselves as tabernacles of the Divine. The ark of the covenant, the Eucharist, the Grand Canyon, and the human soul form one stupendous reality. Religion thus serves to preserve the supremacy of the higher Self and to locate it in nature and in our human hearts. The Song of Songs is a passionate celebration of this triune ratio since it tells of human love in metaphors of nature and does not mention God by name. There is no need. The Divine is understood when the human and the natural are present in full color.

The religious attitude toward the world includes a trust in an immortally loving intent behind every twist of fate. Such trust evokes an unconditional yes to the conditions of existence. It also helps us access and express our unique gifts. Creativity, for example, is an existential capacity, a response to a force that taps on any shoulder. It is not simply a trait of some special people. When big faith taps us that way, it becomes a key to becoming who we *fully* are. This is how the religious attitude leads to and contributes to individuation—now perceived as world individuation.

True religion is not about superstitions or postulations to cling to. It is a call to activate our wide range of powers. Beliefs are meant to be road signs to acting lovingly, wisely, and helpfully in the face of life's conditions by contributing the rich expanse of our unique potential to the world's woes and challenges. This is how religion is a useful, legitimate, and necessary part of evolution.

The religious instinct is not an epiphenomenon of the brain, but new research shows that the inclination toward religion and its rituals are located in a specific brain center. We did not learn to be religious. We are religious by nature. Religion is as deeply imprinted in human nature as the instinct for survival. In 44,000 BCE, a cave man left hyacinths, symbols of resurrection, on the grave of a friend. The pollens remained with the excavated bones and were found recently. Something untaught in the human heart always believed in the transcendence of death, that is, in a reality beyond appearances. A religious instinct in us always believed that rituals made contact with that something. The hyacinth that came back to life from the grave in which it was laid must have given the clue to the potential of rebirth in death. The Divine was perhaps suspected to be the mediating force that fostered such resurrections. Perhaps the triune ratio—human/natural/divine—was budding in the spiritual gardens of our first parents.

The sacred and the profane were not antagonists in the past. Psychological and religious experiences were all one. The split between them happened when knowledge first lost its connection to religion and entered the realm of science only. As whole beings, our psychology cannot be separated from our religious instinct, that is, our inclination to design beliefs, rituals, morality, and devotion as our response to intimations of the Divine.

We have set ourselves the task of investigating our spiritual yearnings in the light of our religion. This involves an ongoing dialogue between psychology and religion as well as both Western and Eastern spirituality. Our work is to distill what is truly catholic from the layers and accretions that have entered over the centuries. The collective experience of humankind is the history of the human psyche and is sacred history. Our most basic need to be human is described in that story. It entails a passover from the limits of a scared, arrogant, or retaliatory ego to a generous Self of love, wisdom, and healing power. The Divine is the foundation, source, and ultimate destiny of this paschal mystery, this passover from death to life. Jesus is the fore-runner and exemplar of it. Every age provides models of the virtues we are meant to practice. For instance, St. Clement of Alexandria acknowledged in his *Stromata* that Buddha had "extraordinary holiness."[10]

Trusting synchronicity means trusting that our past figures into our personal destiny in some unique way. To be born a Catholic means that that fact figures into how one's personal destiny will be fulfilled, and how one's spiritual potential will be best accessed and activated. In fact, our religion is part of who we are and what makes us unique. It has values and truths that speak to us in personal terms, no matter how empty of meaning it may have become for us. It is crucial flora along the landscape of our path. Nothing in our life story was meant to be wasted or jettisoned. Spiritual evolution means continuity with our past and finding the riches in it, familiarly, culturally, educationally, and religiously. Disparagement of ancient mythic motifs deprives us of a living and coherent vision of our roots. Since Christian and all human archetypes and motifs are the same, disparagement of one repudiates the other.

Finally, religion is associated with authority, usually patriarchal authority. However, it does not have to be that way. Over the centuries people have found alternatives. A new, more open style of religion appeared in pre-Christian and Christian Rome. They were called "mystery religions." The popularity and rapid expansion of these mystical cults explain how ready people were for Christianity. In fact, St. Paul refers to Christianity as a mystery religion: "The mystery that has been hidden throughout the ages and generations but has now been revealed to his saints" (Col 1:26).

A mystery religion, or school, is based on initiation, a choice and commitment, rather than being passed on to someone at birth. Examples are the mysteries of Demeter at Eleusis, the mysteries of Mithras in Rome and throughout the empire. A mystery religion differed from Roman imperial and Jewish religion in that it

Offered personal experience of the Divine in relation to the human; something not found in pagan rituals;
Taught that rituals of initiation could transform a person's life and introduce a person to deeper meanings in the cosmos and in personal experience;
Showed how anyone could actually feel an unbrokered connection with the Divine, that is, without priestly mediation;
Taught ways to identify with a divinity through rituals;
Showed how commitment to the gods/goddesses could lead to a sense of private morality, not just public ethics;
Showed how to cultivate a devotion that made the gods personal; and
Taught that the gods loved the initiates personally.

We see this personal dimension also in the prophet Jeremiah, who speaks of a new covenant between God and individuals rather than only to the nation. This more personal sense of what religion can be is an example of finding bigness in one's belief system. Now God is not far away on Mount Olympus, but accessible to those willing to find him.

I beheld nothing but the divine power in a manner assuredly indescribable, so that through excess of marveling, my soul cried out with a loud voice: "This world is full of God!" —St. Angela de Foligno

RECLAIMING OUR POWER

Paradoxically, in order to grow beyond an old myth, it is often necessary to accept the role it played in your life, and understand the reasons you at one time embraced it. —David Feinstein and Stanley Krippner

We notice the changing name of the Church. The word *Roman* was not added until the seventeenth century as the papacy became more prominent. Catholicism then seemed to be mostly about adherence to Roman authority, while the law of Christ's love seemed reserved for saints. The word *catholic,* however, means "universal and all-inclusive." The Church is meant to be catholic in the sense that it is committed to universal love.

The Church is also catholic in ways like these:

It honors and draws from all traditions.

It accommodates, welcomes, and encourages the advances of science and current spiritual consciousness. This is big-minded faith.

It is continually updating itself in the four realms of religion: its beliefs are not tied to outmoded dogmatic formulations; its morality is not rigid but pro-human; its rituals are intelligible and relevant to contemporary people; its devotions are theologically based and not superstitious or magical.

These examples show how religion gains bigness beyond a tie to one city with one perspective. A majority of modern people are not likely to embrace politically incorrect limits, although they might remain Catholic in name. We do not leave what includes us. The more the Church can treat women and gay people as equals, the more it shows its bigness and how its arms are those of an all-embracing Christ, a cosmic Christ indeed. We can also hope for a new style of leadership, not top-down, but horizontal, respectful of the wisdom that emerges from dialogue. Ironically, the reason people cease being Catholic may be because the Church ceases to be catholic.

A truly catholic, that is, universal, attitude is transphilosophical and transinstitutional. That is the meaning of "that all may be one." It is not that all traditions have to fold into Catholicism, but that anyone can become truly catholic, that is, universal, in his or her respect for truth. This reflects the style of evolution. It is not toward uniformity, but toward synthesis. The criterion for a healthy religious attitude is one that unites all traditions without having to abandon one to join another. Traditions are not adversarial but complementary. Theologian John Dunne says, "When one is no longer concerned about reaching agreement and restoring confidence in one's own culture, life, and religion, but simply about attaining insight and understanding, then one can enter freely into other cultures, lives, and religions and come back to understand one's own in a new light."[11]

The complex relationship between human and divine can no longer be mediated by any single voice or tradition. Awareness of the great varieties of the spiritual life has grown too great to permit such limitation. Carl Jung is certainly a great help to us in this respect. He shows us how myths and religious images reflect our deepest identity. He helps us appreciate our inner life as a reflection of the Divine. St. John of the Cross boldly states this wonderful mystical realization: "All the things of God and the soul are one in participant transformation; and the soul seems to be God rather than the soul, and is indeed God by participation."[12]

Some of us remember painful moments in our Catholic past, including abuse. Old injunctions may be nagging at us. It is perfectly normal to be assailed from time to time with anger, shame, and fears that were conditioned into us in childhood. Everyone has automatic trains of thought that link immediate experience with an old belief, for example, "I'll go to hell if I do this." Such fleeting thoughts may never disappear altogether. They do not harm us unless we become obsessive about them or lose our serenity to suit them. A healthy person recognizes such relics as part of his/her mental territory, given the misinformation, superstition, and fears originally drilled into our minds when we had no defense against them. School, parents, the media, and many other sources of influence affected us in the same way.

As adults, we might still feel guilty about innocent pleasure, or so it seems. It could be that some of our guilt is not about pleasure, but about *power.* We have dared to defy the authority who proscribed certain behavior and whom we believe we are supposed to respect for fear of reprisals. We have stepped out of line, taken power into our own hands. To do this is scary because it entails risking the loss of approval or endangering our means of survival. Actually, we have explored or exposed a part of ourselves that reveals us to ourselves. We have come to the frontier of a new identity: one that allows us to say no to an external voice in favor of an inner intuitive voice. Identity for adults begins precisely at the point at which blind obedience to external imperatives comes to an end and baby steps beyond the safe horizons begin.

A common theme in myths is of the hero or heroine who enters the secret room, opens the locked box, or eats the forbidden fruit of knowledge. This knowledge is power and reclaiming it may be what scares us most of all. The hero is the personification of our urgent desire to individuate no matter what it may take or whom it may defy.

Our religious training may have included negations of personal power. We can now ask ourselves whether any of the beliefs listed below are recognizable in our present thought processes. Are any of them traceable to abuses from our religious past?

- I have no real power.
- I will never be able to face anything alone.
- What I need is out there, not at all in me.
- My feelings, my sexuality, my body, and my impulses are dangerous.
- I come second in everything.
- I cannot trust my inner voice.
- I am not allowed to have my own wishes and needs nor to fulfill them.
- I am selfish as long as I try to be independent.
- My purpose in life is to endure pain, not to be happy.
- I do not really know what to do, how to take care of myself, or what I really need.

Grief work releases us so that new affirmations emerge:

- I have the power to face the losses and abuses of my past.
- I express my grief with the full range of my feelings, especially sadness, anger, and fear.
- I trust that grace will transform my sadness into letting go, my anger into forgiveness, and my fear into love.
- I parent myself by allowing my feelings their full career whenever they arise, then letting go, and moving on.
- I am thankful for the grace that has helped me recover from my past and recover its riches.
- I have full permission to live in accord with my deepest needs and wishes, to say no to abuse and yes to happiness.

My joy is the realization that my capacity to love remained intact no matter what happened to me.

Self-negation is associated with guilt. As faith becomes more big-hearted, we experience appropriate guilt but less and less neurotic guilt. Big-hearted faith sets us free from shame and self-blaming. Appropriate guilt is based on a break with one's own conscientious integrity, our shortcoming or misdeed is admitted, amended, and let go of with a commitment to change. Neurotic guilt may or may not be based on true reprehensibility, is or is not admitted, is or is not amended or let go of.

Appropriate guilt is based on accountability; neurotic guilt is based on fear. Neurotic guilt becomes an obsession with an underlying sense of self-shame and serves no purpose. Appropriate guilt serves the purpose of clearing up something, redressing a wrong, rebalancing an imbalance with full accountability. It is a process that ends with a sense of having made progress personally and spiritually. Neurotic guilt is an interrupted process with no resolution or evolution. When faith is big-hearted, we no longer abuse ourselves with neurotic guilt but are free to live unrestrainedly and responsibly.

We free ourselves from guilt in a paradoxical way. We form a healthy and consistent conscience with a firm resolve to make amends when we fail. Then we have a way of processing guilt and transforming it. It is human and is not meant to vanish but to be a signal for correction. Frances Wickes writes, "If there is true self love, the judge becomes the redeemer, and the sense of judgment is lost in the miracle of transformation."[13]

Morality means raiding the stores of love and dissolving the citadel of ego, the essence of psychological sanity and of spiritual sanctity. For an adult, there is less accent on rules and more on the rule of love. We act from joyful choice with great latitude and self-forgiveness. When faith is real, it gives us flexibility and freedom. In fact, "the freedom of the children of God" is the best indicator of a living faith.

As faith matures, motivation for moral living changes from fearful obligation to loving choice. Fear is transformed into love. We no longer act or choose not to act because of the dread of the loss of heaven and pains of hell. We act lovingly because we have come to realize that love is our very identity. Love has no motive; it is all we can do. When we love, we are being ourselves. "God is love" then becomes experientially true and, at the same time, a metaphor for our higher Self than ego. We are identifying with Christ: "My I is God; I have no other me," says the mystic St. Catherine of Genoa. She experienced the continuity of humanity and divinity as is between mind and universe.

In big-hearted faith, the trustful bond of faith is to a God of love and mercy, not to a God of judgment and punishment. St. Anselm's proposition was that God forgives only when he receives full satisfaction for sin. This archaic view can yield to one that certifies God's unconditional love, prompting forgiveness before restitution. In other words, a person who is mature in faith feels unreservedly loved as he/she is, before, during, and after sin. Likewise, there is no retaliation from God, only an offer to us of transformation.

Faith is the courage to accept our acceptability despite feelings of unacceptability.

—Paul Tillich, *The Courage to Be*

CHAPTER TWO

How Faith Expands Us

The only reason that can decide me to adhere to a religion must...consist in the harmony of a higher order which exists between that religion and the individual creed to which the natural evolution of my faith has led me.

—Pierre Teilhard de Chardin, *Christianity and Evolution*

Most of us began our life of faith in childhood. We were introduced to beliefs and to a community of believers. We may thereby have formed a durable bond to the Church. This bond was established before we could say no to it. However, this enduring bond to religion can always be the foundation of a spiritual path or make a contribution to it. Whatever remains alive in our psyche does so because it can contribute in some way. We are given a lifetime to find out how.

This religious bond can go on uninterruptedly, even when we reject childhood beliefs or membership in a church. It is beyond personal control or choice. This is why it is not yet real faith, which is free and can be consciously chosen and rechosen. Mature faith is a yes when we are free to say no.

A lasting bond may be called an *essential* bond. It is like the bond in an intimate relationship. We are bonded in our long-standing love for each other, in our history together, and in our commitment to each other. Yet, all these qualities can remain true while a couple is getting a divorce. For a relationship to work, these unconditional qualities have to be balanced by *existential*—here and now—conditions of love and commitment shown in action. The essential bond requires an existential commitment if there is to be a living bond.

Here are three examples of essential bonds:

The Bond of Memory: This is a remembered sense of warmth, belonging, and security. It is usually based on "how good it felt" to be in church or at religious rituals. This bond is responsive to images, words, fragrances, and tastes. It is comforting and sense-oriented, granting a refuge from the demanding conditions of existence or from our own predicaments. Such consolation may become an avoidance of direct confrontation with our personal challenges and responsibilities. Usually, it is simply a good feeling with little effect on our decisions. This is why it is insufficient as a foundation for a full religious commitment.

The Bond of Superstition: This is an attachment to beliefs and fears that remains in us below the level of rationality. It can account for a continuing sense of guilt and shame, usually with a repertoire of ritual behaviors that are meant to diffuse it. This bond is based on how scary the world is and how crucial it is to know the techniques that make it safe. It is the bond of moralism and legalism, for example, "I have to wear this medal or go to Mass or else I am in danger." Abraham Maslow seemed to describe this bond: "Most people lose or forget the subjectively religious experience, and redefine religion as a set of habits, behaviors, dogmas, and forms which, at the extreme, becomes entirely legalistic and bureaucratic, conventional, empty, and in the truest meaning of the word, anti-religious."[1]

The Bond of Experience: This bond is founded on a personal experience of the transcendent, a felt sense of a personal relationship with Christ or God. Such a bond can exist without personifications like God or Christ and be oriented to a world spirit, nature, or simply a higher power. This bond can occur within a believing community or individually. It can refer to one experience that was powerful and unforgettable, to a series of experiences, or to a long-lasting continuum of experience.

St. Thomas Aquinas wrote, "In the last resort all that we know of God is to know that we do not know him since we can be sure that the mystery of God surpasses human understanding." He became a mystic after his vision of Jesus. He said that all his theological speculation was "as straw," compared to the experience of Christ in person.

Most of us have all three of these bonds operating in us, though the first and second may be most in evidence. For instance, we may not have gone to church in years. Yet when we are thrown off-balance in a crisis, we feel the need to pray or to visit a church. This may be a signal that the bond of memory of our religious past still rekindles a consoling sense of safety, something we feel good going back to.

We may find ourselves feeling guilty about a harmless pleasure, proscribed in our religious past. We may light a candle at a shrine for a relative who is in danger of death. These reactions may signal the bond of superstition.

(Lighting candles prayerfully is an age-old legitimate ritual that becomes a superstition when we believe it works magically, that is, obliges God to respond.)

Finally, we may have an abiding or sudden sense of the presence of the Divine in the silent woods or at the birth of a child. This may be a sign of the bond of experience. A mature personal bond to Jesus means having his heart in us, a heart of courage for our journey and of love for other beings on their journeys. Our declaration may sound like this: "I have a personal relationship with God not only because I talk to him but because I act like him and for him in this world. I am the way he feeds the hungry, clothes the naked, comforts the afflicted." In this bond, Christ may be a personification of the eternal Self, summoning us to tell our life story in the language of unconditional love.

Any essential bond, either by memory, superstition, or relationship, links us to the Church of our childhood but it may not sustain a life of faith in the present. That happens only when the essential bond is joined to an existential commitment: a living, day-to-day responsiveness to the life and teachings of Christ and to his revolutionary values. This is what is meant by putting faith into practice, the only kind of faith that is real.

An existential commitment is an ongoing life history of personal choices to live the divine life in one's here-and-now existence. The essential bond is formed in the past; the existential commitment is renewed in the present. The essential bond is a given; the existential commitment is a choice. Considering all three bonds, an existential commitment is most likely to happen in the context of the bond of experience.

A person may leave the Church and still notice the presence of an essential bond many years later. This is not faith, but a historical vestige of connection to the Church. At the same time, a person can leave the Church and still make decisions that center around the gospel message. This shows faith without active Church membership. Likewise, one can remain in the Church all one's life with an essential bond of memory or superstition with no existential commitment to back it up.

The challenge is to acknowledge the kinds of bonds we hold. Then we may choose to form or solidify a bond of experience and translate it into a here-and-now commitment to faith in action. We receive a message, trust its legitimacy, and then commit ourselves to live in accord with the message in a community of faith or individually. All this takes grace but that grace is available at any time in life.

Some of us carry around antiquated images of faith and the Church. We imagine that these archaic models and beliefs accurately represent the present Church. But our models may be anachronisms, half-truths, or even beliefs the Church once held but no longer holds in the same way. One of the first issues for an adult who chooses to examine his or her faith is to distinguish between the images and recollections of childhood belief and the living message of faith here and now.

WHAT IS FAITH?

Richard McBrien notes that "faith is personal knowledge of God in Christ, that acceptance and knowledge are always achieved and activated within a given community of faith."[2] Thus faith is not simply cognitive but heartfelt. It is not the opposite of experience but directly related to it.

Once one has faith in God, one believes that faith itself is a gift of God. It is not of human making nor can it be produced by effort. It comes by grace; it is received, not achieved. Faith only happens beyond what the mind can conjure. It transcends the limits of ego and intellect. At the same time faith seeks understanding. We keep exploring faith and belief to grow in appreciation of its depth and meaning. This helps faith evolve but does not create or increase it. It remains a part of the gift dimension of life waiting to be opened. The Kabbalah says, "He who reaches out is reached."

Faith leaves room for free choice since it offers no incontrovertible evidence. Nothing about it is absolute or perfectly clear. Scientific knowledge is based on predictable, repeatable, ineluctable evidence. One has to assent. Faith is beyond that which is scientifically provable. Thus faith is itself a bravely transcendent and subversive act because it leaps beyond reason. Faith has no need for evidence.

True faith combines all human opposites and thus even includes doubt. Faith is a lifespan reality, evolving as we evolve, sometimes by regular progress, sometimes by a quantum leap, sometimes by a long absence, and sometimes by a crisis of confidence and doubt.

There is also a personal and community dimension to faith. This does not have to entail membership in a church. We can act with compassion and love in solidarity with our fellow humans whether or not we are members of an institution. In other words, faith is real within a church community or within the human community.

Big-hearted faith does not mean simply holding on to the consoling images of the past as in the bond of memory. That may feel like faith but may only be loyalty. Even after losing contact with the Church, we can be holding onto traditions and images that still have the power to comfort us.

A poignant example of this appears in the book and film *The Lonely Passion of Judith Hearne.* She has "lost" her faith and, while looking at her familiar picture of the Sacred Heart, she says, "Is this the only You there is?" Then when the picture is on the mantle, she adds that it gives her so much comfort.

In the story of Judith Hearne, God has become only a consoling image, a link to the past with no renewed dedication to animate it on a daily basis. Having faith means that the word *God* now denotes our experience of the Divine. It too is a metaphor for a mystery that cannot be limited by words, concepts, or even individual experiences. Nicholas of Cusa presented an allegory for God as a circular sea with no loss of water and a spring in the center that is ever-surging. That does not sound limitable by concepts or dogmatic formulations. The vast psychic ego-transcending aliveness in humankind and in nature is the experience of God. Throughout history at least three perspectives of faith in God have endured:

1. God is a personification of a mystery that defies conceptualization. In this approach, God is a metaphor for a transpersonal mystery, not the mystery itself, but a vehicle to it. If the metaphor is symbolic only in the literary sense, faith does not seem to be present. In ancient times, some philosophers believed that the gods were mere reflections of our own human nature. This is a reduction that nullifies the reality of the transcendent reality beyond ego. A living metaphor is one that affirms this underlying reality. Jungian, eastern, and mystical perspectives fit here.

2. God is the person of the mystery, the mystery in person. In this approach, God is not a metaphor but a person. One can stop here with no need for religion or one can be a member of a believing community. This is deism, faith in a personal god that may not include beliefs, moral positions, rituals, or devotion—the components of traditional religion.
3. The personal God reveals himself and reveals a way to live here now and to go on living hereafter by participation in the mystery, mediated through membership in a faith community and its rituals. When the mystery includes the incarnation and resurrection of Jesus Christ, the response is Christian faith. When that response is congruent with action, it is faith in practice. The Church is a community of believers who participate in sacraments and are beckoned to love and service. The Second Vatican Council added two emphases: faith is a free gift that invites a free acceptance, and Christian faith exists in Christians whether or not they are within the Catholic tradition: "For all who are led by the Spirit of God are children of God" (Rom 8:14). This is faith in the cosmic Catholic sense.

God has bad press today because it has a male-sounding resonance. It also sounds dualistic, as if God were a supreme separate being beyond human experience. *One God* sounds like a single entity with a perimeter. Actually, *God* can refer to the space between the concepts of God. The issue is not whether God *is* but whether he is nothing more than what we have heard about him literally, for instance, whether God is a *he*! Since devotion is an important feature of religion, it is understandable that the terms *Father* or *Lord* were used throughout history. Devotion leads to comfort and security and that is associated with a father or lord who protects us.

There is no single universal signature, only individually unique ones. There is no single love, only each person's brand in giving and receiving it. There can be no single image of God, only individual experiences of God.

What people have meant by *God* has taken many forms:

A male spirit in the sky who sees, knows, and influences all
A person who extends or supplements the power of our ego to punish or reward
A loving and consoling friend who helps us
A person who hears and answers prayers and can reverse the conditions of existence in our favor
The Trinity: Father, Son, and Holy Spirit
A principle of providential comfort
A metaphor for a mystery of presence and meaning
A guarantor of ultimate meaning or the ultimate meaning itself
The source and destination of all
The inner life of all things, the deepest reality of all phenomena as well as their purpose
A world spirit, sometimes the same as nature
Love (usually excluding erotic love) and a guarantee of being personally loved
Any combination of the above

In the Jungian perspective explored so far, we might say that God is the wholeness that is impelled by unconditional love, perennial wisdom, and healing power. God lives in the world by the activation of these virtues in us. Incarnation is actualization of the fullest potential and furthest reach of human/divine life. If God is the eternal Self made conscious in our life and lifetime, then we are the necessary midwives for its epiphany. Revelation about God is evolving by and as the light of human consciousness, one person, one life story at a time.

Now the meaning of faith becomes richer. Our faith includes gratitude for the glories of humanity and of nature. This is why faith is such a necessary feature of spirituality. In this sense, faith is a pathway to a fully inhabited life.

There was always a voice of illumined mystics in and out of the Church who proposed that God was not a supreme being above us while nonetheless a personal relationship is possible. In our childhood religious indoctrination, we may not have been granted that option but instead taught to embrace an incontrovertible dualism. What was thereby excluded from divinity was our own humanity, the feminine, nature, and the shadow side. In addition, when holiness is only in a supreme Being over us, then natural things are depleted of their holiness and so is the psyche.

It is certainly a challenge to love God when God is no longer a person in the sky. If we are used to loving people with faces, it will be hard to love God, who is invisible. We can love others and trust the biblical declaration that love of neighbor *is* love of God. Although we may not believe that God is a person, when we love ourselves and others, we love God-in-person. Dorothy Day said, "I really only love God as much as I love the person I love the least."

If faith is a journey, any approach to it that is phase-appropriate makes sense. We may first believe in a separate person God literally, and later as a metaphor of the transcendent life of all humanity. The first three kings in the Old Testament, Saul, David, and Solomon, exemplify three dimensions of faith development: Saul lives in fear of the literal God; David has devotion to a personal God; Solomon sees God less literally and evolves a humanistic faith.

Nicodemus in the Gospel of John responds to Christ's statement that we be born again in a way that shows he is a literalist. He asks Jesus how a person can be born again since he can't reenter his mother's womb (John 3:4). In the same Gospel, the woman at the well, when offered "living water," that is, grace, takes it to mean actual water (John 4). But Jesus is using a metaphor, the only in-depth way to describe the spiritual life since it is so full of paradoxes.

When children are taught to take a belief or story as literal, there is a danger that in adulthood they will reckon their religion as a fairy tale.

When the moral teachings are anti-body, anti-joy, and inhibiting, people will scuttle them when they grow up.

Rituals that are not fully participatory and alive do not nurture us.

When children are not shown how to establish and rejoice in a relationship to Jesus, they may not find an ongoing place for him in their lives.

Within these same four components of religion, it is possible to

Find ways to appreciate the metaphorical power in the good news story;
Combine healthy psychology with our morality;
Find the deeper meanings in participatory ritual; and
Relate to Jesus as our divine friend and loving companion.

This approach fosters a faith that is vibrantly alive and can remain significant for a lifetime. It is sustainable faith. It comes not from religious instruction but religious arousal. This is the bigness to which religious dialogue, rather than simply instruction, can lead us.

Religious metaphors are ultimately comparisons about the deeper reality of ourselves, our spiritual identity, and our names as "writtten in heaven," to recall a metaphor used by Jesus. A living metaphor is an experience, not just a literary device. It identifies and deepens how we feel the impact of reality. Actually, every metaphor is about the higher, bigger life in us, the true Self beyond ego.

For instance, "March comes in like a lion and goes out like a lamb" seems to express only the weather conditions of the month of March. Yet, it is also about a human style of evolution. The inflated ego enters the world with force and then may be humbled and become more gentle. Some men go into relationships like lions and, as their egos get their comeuppance, they soften and become more sensitive. What seems a trite literary device is a living portrait of how the human organism is made. It follows that there is a spiritual meaning too: the lion lies down with the lamb.

The religious quest for meaning in metaphor widens our consciousness and frees us from the limits of a purely rational or egocentric view of the universe and ourselves. We come to appreciate mystery, not try to cancel it.

A NEW WAY OF KNOWING

The foundation of faith is surrender to ultimate meaning, not to demonstrable fact. Faith draws us into the transcendent mystery of our own and the world's existence. It is necessary for the full range of our knowledge of appearances and what lies beyond them. No single science or combination of all sciences (including noetic and extrasensory ones) adequately expresses the variety and depth of reality. Faith posits that there is a reality that transcends fact, proof, nature's ordinances, and sensory cognition. It is neither objective nor subjective but transcendent. It proclaims that reality is richer than science or intuition can contain.

A fundamentalist believes Christ rose from the dead in the sense that his inanimate, dead body was animated with new life. A nonbeliever says this never happened. Neither one of these statements is about faith. The former posits belief in a palpable and intelligible event; the latter denies that such an event occurred. Both base their view on whether or not the original event actually happened in a material sense. If the "believer" found out that the event did not literally occur, he or she would no longer believe. If the atheist found out and accepted that the event did occur, he or she would believe. In both instances, the perceived authenticity of an event joins with one's acceptance of it to create belief or disbelief. In both instances, the inner assent is founded on the linear historical actuality of a fact. This is scientific knowledge, not faith, because it is based on proof of an ontological reality. When religion is about proving we are right or that mysteries are not really mysterious, we miss out on the wonderful dimensions of divine wisdom and divine surprise. When someone says, "I do not believe in God," he may mean, "I do not believe in the personification of God or this version of God or a God in the sky."

We can accommodate many ways of knowing, not only the one that is based on provable, incontrovertible fact. The following are some examples:

- "I know you have money because I see the cash." *Knowledge through proof has led to certitude.*
- "I know George Washington was the first president because I trust the records of history, even though I cannot prove it as easily as I can prove that my driver's license is real." *Knowledge through acceptance of historical tradition with no thorough chance at proof has led to certitude.*
- "I know my son loves me because I feel it but I cannot prove it." *Knowledge through experience with no possibility of scientific proof has still led to certitude.*

In attempting to know the resurrection in any of these three ways, we may be looking for (1) a certitude based on a physical proof, (2) trust in tradition, or (3) personal memorable experience. But faith transcends all these and posits another element: an inner sense or knowledge that is self-validating: I believe because I believe. It is true because it is true. There is an analogy in Carl Jung's approach to dream images. He says that they are not symbols of something beyond themselves. They refer to themselves. They are self-validating. They stand for and proclaim their own deepest meaning.

The scientific provability of the original events in Jesus' life is relevant only to those who cannot surrender their attachment to logic and proof. As Meister Eckhart says, "The only way to live is like the rose which lives without a why."[3] Furthermore, St. Paul never mentions any event or miracle of Jesus. Christ consciousness is not about that man who lived in Galilee and all his wonders. It is about us and the shape and challenge of our capacity for divine life, the good news of Christ.

Actually, the certitude of faith coexists with a defiance of the way things are known in the linear world. It is not that the events of faith are ambiguous; it is that they are *more* knowable than any rational or intuitive mode of knowing can accommodate. They take place in sacred time and space (unlimited), no longer in secular time and space (limited). They are spiritual events, not merely physical events. The realm of faith is not the realm of news headlines but of an altogether new and mysterious way things happen. Faith is an untutored leap into an unknown reality. It is an initiation, not a logical conclusion. This is why it calls for a surrender.

How do we respond to this statement: "I can't be a Christian because I can't believe Christ rose from the dead in any miraculous way"? We might say that faith is not about how Christ was reanimated from death to life but about how an altogether different way of living happened to him and how that is possible for us too. The fact of resurrection is the fact of a new way of being alive, not a reversal of a physical condition. We are in another dimension unknown to the mind. That is the mystery, an initiation into a way of knowing that cannot be defined in the usual way. In the Gnostic view, only a few have access to the knowledge; in Christianity it is open to all of us.

Faith brings us into a reality, for example, the resurrection, that did not happen in the usual way. It is known only by assent, since there is no paradigm for it in the intellect. If one was standing guard at the tomb when this event occurred and saw it, one would still need faith. A Roman guard could not know the resurrection any better than a present-day believer knows it. Its validity has nothing whatsoever to do with what one saw or could prove. The resurrection appearance stories all have the faith of the respondents in common. Even though they saw, they knew by faith, that is, they discovered a new way of knowing at the same instant that they discovered Christ has a new way of being alive, and this aliveness will never end. The historic event was the bridge to a transhistorical meaning, known and knowable only by faith.

"Alive" can't be a notion; it can only be experiential. In every age, including today, people have experienced Jesus as alive. That is undeniable. In this sense, Jesus *is* risen indeed. People of faith see him as alive whether or not all people experience him that way. Another example of the uniqueness of Christ is that his story presents the full expanse of the human journey archetype from death to resurrection, from the first moment of creation to the final moment of time. This is not the usual heroic journey archetype of finding a higher consciousness and sharing it with others or rescuing others from dangers. The Christ story has themes that encompass the entire breadth and depth of all that humans can expect in a spiritual life: the divine/human, matter/spirit, death/resurrection, earthly/ascended, suffering/redemption, and ordinary/transfigured. In addition, this is not just a story we can follow and whose hero we can imitate. The risen Christ offers us the graces to pursue his path, something that ordinary heroes cannot provide. In all these ways, the story, life, and promises of Jesus deserve attention from anyone who has a spiritual orientation.

This same principle operates with respect to the specialness of Christ's presence in the Eucharist. In a laboratory, the host is still bread. However, it has an enduring living *sacramental reality* that is immeasurable and invisible to the naked eye and to the microscope. This sacramental reality is visible to the eye of faith. Faith in the presence of Christ in the Eucharist is based on a change in the *kind* of reality it is.

Faith not only posits a transformation but even a new way of being real, one that transcends and defies linear objective science. The eucharistic Christ in bread is not fact in the measurable historical sense; it is fact in the immeasurable historic sense. (*Historical* refers to what happened; *historic* refers to the significance of what happened). To believe in the Real Presence is to believe Christ is really present and that there is a way of being present (sacramentally) that is more real than physical presence. The laws of science and nature are not acceded to here. To believe or to posit another mode of being is not just another way of knowing.

Faith is not meant to be supported by proof. Faith is about *another way truth happens.* The risen Christ and the eucharistic presence of Christ represent new ways of being real. The assent of faith is to this *other* reality that transcends finite being and beings. Something is alive beyond the merely living. Living things die; the new kind of life does not end in death but ends death. This is why faith is so courageous. It never disparages reality but insists on expanding it. It dares to know another universe that is beyond but also within this one.

> A Compound manner,
> As a Sod
> Espoused a Violet.[4]

Now, we can more clearly understand our original assertion that faith is limited and stunted when it is literally about the facticity of historical events. It actually refers to the archetypal meaning of historic moments in which divine potential became actual.

Authentic religion does not impose itself on us from without; it assists us from within. William James understood that the unconscious acts so powerfully that it can feel like Divine influence. Theology, with its fear of psychological reductionism, distinguishes religious experience from psychic events. But, as we have seen, all religious experience originates and takes place in the human psyche. There is no division, only distinction, what Huston Smith calls "bridges, instead of barriers."[5]

The psychic event of appreciating transcendence or suddenly seeing it, either as a white light or as a homeless woman, is a religious event because it peeks behind the commonest appearances for a more profound reality. We not only see that reality; we become it and become Christ in it. Now we glimpse the luminous meaning in these words of St. Augustine's fifteenth epistle: "The paschal mystery [death and resurrection] is accomplished in its interior and highest meaning in the human heart [interiorly]."

> *Christ's life is not simply a model for how to live, but the living truth of my own existence. Christ is not alive now because he rose from the dead two thousand years ago. He rose from the dead two thousand years ago because he is alive right now.*
>
> —Christian Wiman, *My Bright Abyss*

NO FINAL FORMULATION

In high school, our study of history was presented as a linear story with a beginning, middle, and no end yet. We began with the Stone Age and ended with the most recent war. It all hung together with continuity and coherence. We were given the impression that many things could be like that. The true/false tests we took made it seem that there were absolutes and if we got them right, we would be rewarded.

It is understandable that when we learned about religion, we thought it, too, was also sewn up as one seamless story. It began with the Garden of Eden and ended with the Apocalypse. We were taught a well-reasoned, well-defined set of dogmatic beliefs, moral principles, and a systematic worldview. We were taught that we were all here for a specific spiritual purpose—"To know, love, and serve God in this life and be happy with him in the next." We were shown the tools to achieve that purpose, for example, believe in the tenets of the Creed, obey the Commandments and Church precepts, receive the sacraments, and trust in grace. As with our school introduction to history, we thought it all made sense as an unchanging, reliable, and consistent whole. We presumed that, since there was an unaltered clarity in the *formulation*, there was a similarly neatly delineated set of beliefs behind it. For us, the format of the teaching was synonymous with the way truth works—as absolute.

Then came the Second Vatican Council, and we realized that there could be a new version of the story. However, we then thought that the new formulations were simply an upgraded but nonetheless still coherent outline of what salvation is about. We still did not quite understand that the Council was the first in our lifetime, but certainly not the last in history. We may not have grasped that the new and central insight was that there is no final formulation, that there will never be a firmly laid out story about God and us. We still had not dared to believe that our religion could be so vibrant and moving not to stop at any final definition.

We now realize that a Church that has a Holy Spirit that blows where it will does not permit a fully concluded declaration of faith. It will always be under construction. That is what makes it so real. Faith is like a cathedral. It looks like it was finished in the Middle Ages, but actually it is being upgraded, altered, and remodeled daily. It is never done; there is no final version. That is a sign that it is a living experience, not simply a structure of stone.

To return to our school analogy, we might say that religion is like science class, not history class. We can read our old history book and learn from it. Our seventh-grade science book has inaccurate information for today. (Actually, even the study of history is being upgraded as we gain new ways of understanding the past.)

Religion is not like the times tables, which remain as is for a lifetime. It is like the dictionary, which presents new words and omits old words all the time. It certainly always contains the English language, but its line-up of words is ever renewing itself. That is analogous to religion. It is basically the same while also variegated—one and many simultaneously. No one can stop it midsentence and say, "This is it!" There will always be more, since religion is ever transcending itself, like everything else in the universe.

It is important not to expect to have a full coherent vision in our minds about our religion. No catechism can contain it all; it is too big and too evolutionary to permit finality. Our theology is always provisional, like science. It can't be boxed or fixed in a single frame. Revelation is a living, ongoing reality, not a letter sent on Pentecost with the only and final directions to heaven.

There is no conclusive, definitive version in our minds, or in any mind, of what or who God is, of who Christ is, of what salvation is, of what any doctrine is fully. Faith is a journey into mystery, not an arrival at logical certitudes. We can only continue to contemplate, to open to new trends in theology, to engage in dialogue with others, and to wonder at the infinite variability of our existence in God's heart. Our religion has infinite range but can't be fenced in.

Pierre Teilhard de Chardin, in a prayer written to his cousin Marguerite, gave this advice: "Accept the anxiety of feeling yourself in suspense and incomplete."[6] It is normal to feel exactly that about our faith. Religion is not like the story of *Hamlet.* It is like the *meaning* of *Hamlet.* The story is the same and will remain the same. The meaning does not change, but it does keep *opening* in new ways in every generation and will continue to do so. There won't be, nor can there be, a final interpretation that declares its precise significance for all time.

All of this refers to the framework of story and belief we carry in our minds and hearts. For that, there can be no final formulation or interpretation. However, when it comes to faith as experience, there may very well be an enduring, consistent sense of God's presence in our lives. *How* this presence makes itself known may change throughout our lifespan, but the *fact* of the presence remains. An example for many of us is the presence of Christ in the Eucharist: our understanding of *how* he is present may change, but *that* he is present abides. What matters most is that faith is experiential rather than notional.

Each of us has unique revelatory moments of that which is More, Beyond, Transcendent, God. The stories of biblical characters and saints introduce us to their experiences, in accord with their time and culture. It follows that it is up to us to present our experience in accord with our time and culture. Being an institutional expression of the transcendent experience, the Church becomes appealing when it too continually updates itself.

Once we trust the Holy Spirit, we come to love the openness, the budding, blooming, and harvesting styles of faith. It is not tentative but evolutionary. It is not confused, only ever-fusing. We can learn to let go of the old security of one clear take on religion. We then embrace the wonder of a kaleidoscopic faith. The beads are always the same but with every turn there is a new display. That is good news for those who honor the Holy Spirit, who loves our faithful curiosity.

> *Judgment and closure are the greatest dangers to one who wants to retain the psychic mobility of an explorer.*
> —John Lilly

STAGES ON OUR JOURNEY

We receive an inner gift only when we are ready to act on it. This is synchronicity, that is, meaningful coincidence of inner and/or outer events. Jonah refused his prophetic gift and soon learned there was no escaping it. St. Augustine said, "Lord, make me pure, but not yet," and received some extra time. A free gift means permission for a free response.

It takes a long series of steps and shifts to reach self-realization. The old view that all is known and grasped in a childhood catechism no longer seems authentic. We now see that our religious life is more like an evolving itinerary than a static grasp of universal truths. This does not represent a turning away from the spiritual; it is a profound respect for it. It is a recognition that the spiritual journey motif mirrors human processes of transformation: we find ourselves always evolving, changing, and growing in appreciation of truth, yet never quite possessing it.

The hero's journey story is encouraging to faith, since it allows for a period away from religion as part of the process of truly finding it. The journey generally is described as having three phases, which apply to relationships, family, and also careers:

- The phase of security: *Containment* in the beliefs, habits, values, and behaviors of one's past.
- The phase of struggle and doubt: *Departure* from this womb-like comfort to enter the world outside with all its challenges, dangers, and self-confrontations. A "loss of faith" is a legitimate, though not universal, part of this process.
- The phase of returning to reclaim the wealth: *Return* to one's roots with newfound powers: expanded consciousness, greater appreciation of the depth of our original faith with appreciation of metaphor or literality, flexible rather than rigid ways of loving and believing. The story of the prodigal son contains the archetype of what seemed lost but was always there waiting for us.

We may experience the consolation of belonging and then the alienation of rejecting en route to the integration of rediscovering. We respect our timing in each of these three phases, neither rushing to the next one nor shamed for the current one.

In the first phase—containment—we swallow the teachings whole, that is, uncritically and literally. We look for boundaries to be set by others since we have so few of our own. We project moral authority onto others, not yet ready to trust our own consciences. (Boa constrictors swallow their prey whole without chewing. They then cannot move but have to sleep for days while digestion happens!)

In the second phase—departure and struggle—we set clear boundaries and establish our own identity over against the teachings of others.

Finally, in the third phase—reunion and commitment—we find a way to integrate our identity with the teachings.

In each phase, we may begin with no clear boundaries, then set rigid boundaries, then maintain our own boundaries and honor others' boundaries. We are first closely attached, then strongly detached, then united comfortably. Here is a summary of the phases of faith:

Attachment: Childhood: Church as Parent
- Blind faith: *accept without question*
- Swallowing beliefs and moral injunctions whole
- Guilt about what we have done/shame for being who we are
- Blind obedience
- No critical sense or boundaries

Detachment: Adolescence and Young Adulthood: Church as Antagonist
- Doubting: *struggle with questions*
- "Picking and choosing" beliefs or moral standards
- Less guilt
- More struggle and rebellion
- Experimentation outside the accepted norms

Integration: Adult Faith: Church as Supportive Community

Reclaiming archetypal riches and values: *appreciate values and commit to them*
Attention but not necessarily obedience
Appreciation of and commitment to faith in a way that integrates spirituality and psychological maturity

Faith does not have to mean finding our final resting place in unaltering certitude or in any one phase. This would not be faith but fixation. True faith mirrors life; it keeps moving onward, a heroic journey, an evolution from light to dark and back to light. In the fullness of the faith experience, one image of God gives way to another. A lively inner experience of living faith happens when the old containers of faith vanish and new perspectives and challenges arise and are greeted with courage and joy.

To be fixated in the attachment phase makes for regression or fanaticism.
To be fixated in the detachment phase makes for problems with authority and/or alienation.
To move from phase to phase makes for normal faith development.

We are just as much persons of faith when we struggle as when we integrate. Even the undiscerning blind faith of childhood has its place in at least focusing us on the transcendent. The struggle is actually a lifelong process and coexists with the other two phases. We may question even when we swallow whole; we question when we commit to faith.

When we are angry or bitter, we are still in the struggling phase. As long as we are attempting to prove or convince, we are still struggling. As long as we are wrestling with faith questions, we are still struggling. Struggle and doubt do not signify lack of faith. They show the versatile nature of faith and its living quality of evolution.

Only when we land on flatline matter-of-factness are we through with faith: atheism with no interest in further exploration and total indifference to God, faith, or religion. This includes hopelessness, that is, no belief in a purpose to the universe, a calling in every individual life, and an ultimate meaning in all that is.

If we return to an appreciation of the archetypal and moral values of our religious past, though not necessarily to membership in a church, our journey is still complete. We have followed the heroic motif of containment, struggle-oriented departure, and reunion.

Faith also moves through stages like these:

Stage One: Literalism: a one-dimensional view in which God is anthropomorphic and mirrors the human ego for better or for worse. This can be narrow and rigid in the face of the unruly conditions of existence. It is an uncritical assent. The accent is on reliability of authority and blind assent to the rules and dogmas of authority. The loyalty is to the institution rather than to individual inquiry.

Stage Two: The symbolic and abstract take more prominence. There is a personal entry into issues, a greater internal motivation, a commitment to apply personal experience to the design of conscience. Here there may be a crisis of faith and more ambiguity.

Stage Three: A more intuitive approach arises. There is more acceptance of paradox and mystery. One can

> recognize meanings and riches in what was rejected before. The mystery of unity of all things begins to dawn. This unity is about community and is interdependent.

It is difficult to understand or be understood by people too far behind or ahead of us in these stages, so dialogue is difficult. We can only dialogue fully with those at our stage, those who remember the one we are in, or those who are headed for the next one.

Faith means meeting a subject—ourselves in God—rather than finding an object. There is no object after all, since the source of spiritual longing and the goal of it are one and the same. We are always and already in contact with the divine nucleus of our psyche and of our universe. It includes and is yet beyond our ego, "its center everywhere, its circumference nowhere."

ENCOUNTERING THE INSTITUTION

The Church consists in the experience of communion of the whole world. —St. Augustine

In ancient Dodona in Greece, an oak was revered as a source of prediction and prophesy by the local people. Later, when it became famous, it was dubbed an oracle of Zeus by the people and then even by the priests. Still later, what was at first a personal encounter with the tree became off-limits to the public and could only be approached by people through intermediary priests.

This is a paradigm of what can happen to humankind's religious instinct. It begins as a personal encounter with nature where the reality behind its appearances is acknowledged as transcendent. Then it falls into the hands of a patriarchal authority structure, who decides how and to whom its graces will be dispensed. A living Church is not the guard of the sacred oak, but the guardian of the people's right to approach it. The *it* is our inner psyche, nature, and God, all one reality. We recall that Jesus spoke against belief in the necessity of the Jewish priesthood for contact with God. The religion of pagan Rome likewise insisted that priests were required for contact with the Divine. In both instances, the belief supports and legitimates patriarchal authority.

Institutions based on a male authority model are best confronted by solidarity within a group rather than by isolated individuals. We cannot fix the institutional Church, but we can confront its need to fix itself. We cannot shoulder the griefs of the Church, only our own personal experience within it. It also follows that the Church as community can ask us for the same acceptance "all the way to the bottom" that we give to and ask of any human beings we love. The work is, after all, interdependent and interactive. Nathaniel Hawthorne wrote, "Man must not disclaim his brotherhood even with the guiltiest."[7]

The Second Vatican Council chose the title *people of God* in preference to *institution* as a title for the Church. Avery Dulles has proposed five major models: institution, mystical communion, sacrament of Christ, herald of the Gospel, and servant of the world. All these models coexist, although the institutional model has tended to predominate in post-early Church history.

Many of us have an inborn mistrust of institutions. It is easy to think of ourselves in opposition to institutions. We forget that institutions can be contexts for growth. They provide the security of order in which we have room to try our wings, test limits, and explore our options. They sometimes place stops in our way, but they also create steps. This is how the human character develops: through both stops and steps. Our work is to grow in spite of their obstructions and to change them constructively so that they can serve our needs and those of others. This takes working together.

In *The Good Society*, Robert Bellah says,

> It is hard for us to think of institutions as affording the necessary context within which we become individuals; of institutions as not just restraining but enabling us; of institutions not as an arena of hostility within which our character is tested but as an indispensable source from which character is formed. This is in part because some of our institutions have indeed grown out of control and beyond our comprehension. But the answer is to change them, for it is illusory to imagine that we can escape them.[8]

Avery Dulles distinguishes between an institution and institutionalism. An institution is an ordered society that works within a structure of hierarchy and regulations to fulfill a specific set of goals. "By institutionalism we mean a system in which the institutional element is treated as primary.…A Christian believer may energetically oppose institutionalism and still be very much committed to the Church as institution."[9]

An institution is a means to an end. The goal is sufficient order so that one can live and work serenely. Healthy institutions create limits on the leaders. These limits protect the freedom of all. Institutionalism makes the institution an end in itself. Its purpose is to preserve itself at any cost. Its limits inhibit freedom. Person becomes secondary to system. Those in authority are often above the law, at least in their way of seeing themselves.

Yet, ultimately, commitment to any church will entail meeting up with an institution. In fact, even two people joined in marriage become an institution! As noted above, healthy institutions provide a setting in which goals can be achieved. They facilitate movement, dialogue, and change. They help us confront our identity as one-with-many. At the same time, we admire twelve-step programs that are not institutions but are fully successful in creating community, encouraging an appreciation of a higher power, and achieving their members' recovery goals.

Institutionalism happens when the means is confused with the end. An institution bends itself and its habits to fit its ultimate goal. It does not become tied to a single formulation of the truth. It sees itself as in the service of its members. It continually reformulates, redesigns, and reorganizes to keep pace with changing times and needs. It acknowledges every model it may espouse as temporary and discardable in favor of one that is now more fitting. It sees the times change and changes with them. Yet it can be trusted to conserve the timeless in the midst of every vicissitude. "The forms of Buddhism must change so that the essence of Buddhism remains unchanged. This essence consists of the living principles that cannot bear any specific formulation," says Thich Nhat Hanh in words that apply to all churches.[10]

One of the reasons the good news is good is because it includes us all. What we may have been exposed to in Catholicism was not the kerygma—a living, universal, limit-transcending wisdom—but a narrow, male-dominated, fear-driven, and shame-based anti-human burden, "this thing that hath a code but not a core," to use Ezra Pound's words.[11]

William James warned of "faith in someone else's faith." We distinguish personal experience from what is experienced by others and handed to us as mandatory. We all have the privilege of doing what Giordano Bruno, Teilhard de Chardin, and Meister Eckhart did: to come up with our own synthesis. This is part of the work of faith. An adult faith is designed by the individual in the context of the community but not limited by it, especially when it is stuck in atavistic or life-denying beliefs. St. Thomas, Raimondo Panikkar, Thomas Merton, Teilhard de Chardin, and many more show the way.

Faith becomes a community event and churches are formed because good news cannot be kept to itself. The work is to be both a witness and a follower: "It happened to me so I bear witness to the truth of it." The Church is any place where one joins other witnesses and commits to justice, peace, and universal compassion. It is also the place where the glad tidings of our capacity for universal love are honored and are enlisted in the service of others both in and out of the believing community. This growth in moral adulthood that results is personal progress and contributes to the evolution of the entire human community.

There is definitely a move toward new religious structures in America today. The traditional religious forms may not appeal to liberals, but liberal churches are arising among people with higher educations and of higher economic and social class. Among both conservatives and liberals, many are disaffected with institutionalized religion and seek smaller, mutually supportive communities of faith. Some individuals feel no need for mediators and believe they can have a direct experience of the Divine. This is an ancient belief of and quest in the human psyche. Inclusion of Eastern religious views and practices and membership in Eastern religions have grown strongly across America and Europe. Disillusionment with traditional religion has led some to a search for the universal oneness offered in Eastern traditions, especially Buddhism.

In any healthy society, the speculating members at large are ahead of the conservators of the official constitution. Progress usually derives from just such tensions. The issue here is free speech so that change can occur and people can be acknowledged as free, without fear of reprisals for speaking up. The issue then is public versus private, not official magisterium versus theological opinion.

A healthy Church encourages dialogue, not so that others understand its unbending principles, but so teachings can be reformulated in accord with modern needs. When the official Church does this, it acts in accord with its mission of evangelization. Here are two pertinent comments: "Difference is positive only within communion with the other: in respect of the other who is other and yet not alien to us," says Edward Schillebeeckx.[12] Robert Bellah adds, "Disagreements are not so much a failure of consensus as they are evidence of the vigor of a debate over what the Church, and ultimately religion, is all about in our society."[13]

Institutional Religion May	**Spiritually Alive Religion May Offer**
Be authoritarian	Guidance and comfort
Insist on uniformity of belief	Respect for one's unique journey
Be hierarchical, especially between clergy and laity	Equality

(Continued)

(Continued)

Become fear-based: "the loss of heaven and the pains of hell..."	An emphasis on compassion and a consoling sense of a loving intent in the universe
Propose clear-cut dogmas and moral Codes	Evolving beliefs that emerge from rather than suppress dialogue
Insist on membership in an institution	Participatory presence without the need to join something
Hold the keys to the means of grace	Power to find, devise, and expand
Insist that it has all the truth worth knowing	Openness to all traditions

Paul Tillich commented that anyone seeking meaning has religious faith. Bernard Lonergan adds that faith is possible without beliefs. Beliefs are intellectually formed affirmations consequent upon faith. Vatican II emphasized the community dimension of faith, that it happens fruitfully within a believing community. We are touched by the witness of others and so grow in faith, that is, we are moved by the lives of saints. The saints are guides to the wise solutions and loving powers in ourselves. The statues we see in a church represent the potentials in us, realized in them. To light a candle to them is to proclaim the joyous and boundless possibilities in ourselves of the life of faith and service we honor in them.

People look at the institution, the antiquated laws, the repressive strictures and think that the Church is moribund. However, the life of the Church is gauged by the vitality of her saints, the thousands of loving and wise people who live out the works of mercy every day of every year. Their charisms are impervious to institutional repressions or atavistic beliefs. The reliable presence of saints in the world is the evidence of the Spirit at work in time. No institution or rule can interrupt that evolutionary vigor. The Church is as alive today as it was in 100 CE. There are just as many saints and martyrs, just as many teachers, just as many miracles, just as many loving commitments, and just as many living incarnations of Jesus Christ.

When a pope is saintly, as we see in Pope Francis, he becomes the spiritual friend of the earth and of all humanity. The pope archetype carries the ego/Self axis by holding the burden of the opposites: great power and human lowliness. Thus it is a metaphor for our work in the world as servants of it and effective powers in its evolution. The world needs us as servants in humility and as authoritative voices in our pointing to injustice. We are infallible when we speak in loving terms and respond to the needs of our fellow humans. "Your Holiness" is an address to the higher nature of the universe and of all of us. As Marcus Borg and John Dominic Crossan have stated:

> People like Jesus and Paul were not executed for saying, "Love one another." They were killed because their understanding of love meant more than being compassionate towards individuals, although it did include that. It also meant standing against the domination systems that rule their world, and collaborating with the Spirit in the creation of a new way of life that stood in contrast to the normalcy of the wisdom of this world.[14]

THREE HURDLES TO A VIBRANT FAITH

In the Catholicism of our childhood, we might have inherited three religious distortions of Christ's teaching: rejection of Christ's full humanity—which is the rejection of our own humanity; rejection of the power and necessity of grace; and a tendency to view our bodies, our world, and sex with suspicion. These correspond to three specific heresies in the history of the Church: Monophysitism, Pelagianism, and Manichaeism. Each of these exaggerated perspectives needs to be realigned appropriately in big-hearted faith.

The official Church has been slow in the full upgrading of these three old perspectives. We are responsible, as individuals of conscience, to reinstruct and reform ourselves. In our work of recovery of the riches in our religious heritage, it will help to examine these exaggerated views, since they have so often led to dissatisfaction, confusion, and pain.

1. Fearing What Is Human

The engendering of fear in some of us was a sad patrimony of organized religion. We were afraid of our bodies, our freedom, our imagination, our instincts, our passions, and our own potential. To recover the riches of our heritage requires a transformation—salvation—of our ego, caught in fear and desire. It is called to freedom from fear and desire. This is both a grace and a task, that is, it is received by grace and achieved by faithwork. This is our spiritual practice in the context of our religious commitment.

An important step toward an enriched faith is confronting our religious fears. We fear what we have not integrated.

In the fifth and sixth centuries, the Monophysites in

the Eastern Church challenged the Council of Chalcedon (451) by stating that Christ had a divine nature but not a human nature. This view was condemned and the Eastern Church was then interdicted until 519. Though the official Church preserved the orthodox view, *de jure*, throughout the ages, we can see that prior to Vatican II, Christ had been viewed *de facto*, as divine to the detriment of his humanity. This reflects the neo-Platonic emphasis of St. Augustine on God as totally other.

The main deleterious effect was on spirituality, which came to mean "disembodied" and "otherworldly." A prominent emphasis in the Church from St. Augustine (fourth century) to St. Alphonse (eighteenth century) was on freeing the soul from its imprisonment in the body. The glorified body of Christ (postresurrection) was considered our model and goal. An appreciation of the physicality and sexuality of Jesus was noticeably missing in most spiritual writings. This view is also antifeminist because Christ as a model meant a male as a model.

Behind this lurks a fear of women's power and of nature's power. These fears are the results of centuries of refusal to accept the humanity of Christ as fully endorsing our human and natural condition.

The incarnation honors humanness and earthly reality as totally appropriate vehicles for the transcendent. Our transpersonal destiny can only be articulated, embodied, and completed in fully human terms. Yet we have often feared our own humanness, seeing it as inherently wayward and untrustworthy.

True spirituality includes bodiliness. Our bodies are not second best in the spiritual life. They are the best and only vehicles we have to work with on our spiritual path—as on our psychological path. To see Christ only as the Divine

Pantocrator, the distant God, is a denial of the incarnation of Emmanuel, God-with-us, living a shared humanity.

2. Overlooking the Power of Grace

Pelagius (355–425), a British monk, challenged St. Augustine on the issue of free will and predestination. He had some refreshing ideas, but his work was condemned as heretical in 431 by the Council of Ephesus. His main heterodox belief was that grace was unnecessary. People could be saved by their own will and effort. We now understand that Pelagius was not as extreme as people thought he was. For instance, he viewed reason, understanding, and free will as forms of grace. Grace refers to an infusion of power and discernment that exceeds the limits of our will and intellect. It cannot be created or won, but is a free gift of God to humanity, that is, not generated by nature or ego but by a power beyond it.

We all have a fear of trusting grace to come through for us. We inherited the distorted view that all that can be counted on is our own ego, our own bootstraps. Part of growing up in faith is recontacting the Holy Spirit within ourselves, that is, trusting the power of synchronous grace to pull us through—spiritually though not necessarily physically—as long as we act with integrity. We can trust a higher power than our ego, accessible within the depths of ourselves. We then find ourselves acting with consciousness, compassion, and truthfulness. This is the path from grace to effort.

Such trust in grace makes it easier to be witnesses in the world rather than colluders with its values. This path may not safeguard our institutions or even our lives. It guarantees no safety at all. We will have no foothold except the gospel. At risk is everything except truth and vision, the only survival that matters when faith is real. The challenge of faith is always the acknowledgment of an unseen, enduring, and powerful reality behind and despite appearances to the contrary: "We are treated as impostors, and yet are true; as unknown, and yet are well known; as dying, and see—we are alive; as punished, and yet not killed" (2 Cor 6:8–9). St. Paul referred to the Church in his epistles as a local community of committed people who are living in an ego-defying way.

Grace fulfills human nature. Our work is not enough; the endowments of our intellect and will are not enough. Since grace is intrinsic not extrinsic, it is not an addition to our nature but a condition of its fulfillment. Graces are not gained by effort, but given along the path to those who stay on it. Grace does not replace freedom, but fulfills it by releasing our greatest potential. In this sense, grace divinizes human existence.

In grace, the ego is not destroyed but supplemented and transcended. Indeed, Karl Rahner says that grace is indistinguishable from the tendency in the human spirit to transcend ego desire, self-absorption, or fear. To commit ourselves to action is the work we do—implicitly a response of faith. This means acknowledging the power of grace and the inner life as one continuum. No merit can induce grace and yet it is ever-available since God is always sustaining us and always creating us. In fact, creation is grace. Grace is the Self-communication of God. The archetype of this grace is the risen Christ. The giver of grace is the Holy Spirit.

3. Being Caught in Dualism

Mani, a third-century Zoroastrian Persian, was a notable importer of dualism to the West. St. Augustine was a Manichee in his early life but later repudiated it. The Manichees held that the body was evil and the soul good, a Platonic view that paralleled St. Augustine's own. Although Manichaeism was condemned as heretical in the fifth century, its dualistic view of humanity reemerged throughout the Church's history with the Bogomils, Cathari, Albigensians, and Jansenists. Martin Luther was in this same tradition, as were John Calvin and John Knox.

Ever-recurrent dualisms thrived on a belief in sharp divisions between body and soul, matter and spirit—the opposite of a cosmic view. Sex was looked upon with fear. Many saints taught hatred of the body and the value of harsh, unhealthy ascetic practices. The Church became the conservatory and perpetrator of fear and taboo. Pleasure itself was considered sinful if it was indulged in or chosen. This has continued in various forms from St. Augustine's time until the present.

A frightened, narrow view of sex can create a hell on earth for sincerely pious people. The sign of an adult, responsible, and joyous Church is that it fosters happiness "on earth as it is in heaven." Discipline in healthy terms means not indulging the part of us that wants to be hard on ourselves. The warrior is vigilant and exercises continual custody over the archaic organizing principles that are life-negating. But we never choose to harm ourselves.

As mentioned above, until recent times, the linear logical thinking of the scholastic philosophy of the thirteenth century became the paradigm of Catholic theology. The Church's official stand on abortion, birth control, homosexuality, war, and so on, tends to reflect an adherence to a line of logic rather than a respect for the nature of reality. This is why the official moral stance of the Church continually requires upgrading if it is to be taken seriously by people who have found holistic perspectives in life.

An adult believer today can confront dualism in the Church rather than simply reject it. The moral issue then becomes not whether but how behaviors and choices can become more responsible. This creates a context in which normal human behavior and morality are finally integrated (with considerable reduction of neurotic guilt!). A true moral law does not prescribe; it describes. It harmonizes how things can be with how they are. This is the bigness of morality; it embraces diversity as Christ did.

Who, then, is my neighbor? To whom am I bound? Whom must I love?...Love knows no classifications.

—Thomas Merton, *Seasons of Celebration*

CHAPTER THREE

Challenging Conditions on the Spiritual Path

Everything without exception is an instrument and means of sanctification, providing that the present moment is all that matters.

—Jean Pierre De Caussade, SJ,
The Sacrament of the Present Moment

In high school geometry we began the problem-solving of a theorem with givens: axiomatic facts not alterable by us. There are also givens of human existence, circumstances and predicaments that occur in everyone's life. These are the givens that we may have believed it was the task of religion to assuage or even eradicate. However, a mature faith does not reject reality; it addresses it. As part of our spiritual practice, we attend to and accept the givens we keep noticing in life.

The conditions of existence are sources of spontaneity, surprise, unexpected miracles, unpredictable turns of events, creative challenges, and opportunities. The conditions of existence are stimuli for the life force. They are the ingredients of spiritual growth: depth in how we see the world, compassion for all other humans who face the same givens we do, and courage to stand up to change and live through it. This is the very definition of a spiritual hero, one who lives through change, is transformed by it, and then helps others on the path.

The path is threefold, as Reinhold Niebuhr prayed in 1943: "God give us grace to accept with serenity the things that cannot be changed, courage to change the things that should be changed, and wisdom to know the difference."

We work hard to change what can be or needs to be changed. We say yes to the things we cannot change, what is called "the will of God." Our yes is "Thy will be done." Our practice is in imitation of Christ: "In him it is always 'Yes'" (2 Cor 1:19).

This practice is based on trust. Our yes is our way of trusting that whatever happens, no matter how disturbing, is an opportunity for spiritual progress. Big-hearted faith makes room in us to surrender to any given. There are as many givens as there are human predicaments. We can explore five that stand out in a religious context: impermanence, suffering, God permitting evil, our sense of aloneness, and our meeting up with the darkness in the Divine.

EVERYTHING IS CHANGING

The more the future opens before me like some dizzy abyss or dark tunnel, the more confident I may be—if I venture forward on the strength of your word—of losing myself and surrendering myself in you, of being assimilated by your body, Jesus.

—Teilhard de Chardin

The first given of reality is that everything in life is transitory, changing, not permanently satisfying. Nonetheless, we keep attempting to force things to stay the same for us, to last for us. "Abide, thou art so fair," is how Faust said it. We find it hard not to be in control; that is the equivalent of a fear of change. This is a problem for beings like us slated to evolve, that is, to change and grow continually.

We may deny that our humanity contains a bell-shaped curve: rising, cresting, falling. These are the three continually repeated phases that occur in all our attractions and repulsions. The given of transitoriness simply recalls that all things in life pass through stages and curves. We rise in fascination with a thing or place or person or idea. Then we hit a high point and we crest. Finally, our fascination declines. When this happens, the healthy practice is to mourn the loss and move on to what comes next.

When a Roman emperor-elect walked in procession to receive his crown, he was interrupted three times by a slave who lit a quick-blazing flare in his face and said "*Sic transit gloria mundi.*" This same custom carried over to the coronation of a pope. A priest, in unadorned black, stepped between the pope and the pomp, with a lighted flare, and declared, "Holy Father, thus passes the glory of the world."

Life lights that flare for us many times on the grandiose procession that our ego, the attitude of control and entitlement in us, makes through life. Nature balances our inflations with deflations again and again. We can say yes to this or we can use people, places, things, or religion to stave off the inevitable truth of constant change. Adults, people who accede to reality, are at home with the bell-shaped curve and land safely on it.

A person who opposes reality cannot see the inexorable impact of the conditions of existence on himself because his ego is so inflated. He imagines he can conquer them all: never get old and wrinkled, never die, and so forth. Maturity makes a fuller vision possible. That is the equivalent of the egoless view. In other words, letting go of ego makes it possible to be spiritual. It grants us a broader way of seeing and agreeing with reality.

St. Paul wrote, "For we know that if the earthly tent we live in is destroyed, we have a building from God, a house not made with hands, eternal in the heavens" (2 Cor 5:1). Christ said, "Heaven and earth will pass away, but my words will not pass away" (Matt 24:35). Religious statements like these speak to our terror about transitoriness. Every given is a terror to those who do not greet the cycles of life and death with equanimity. The promise that death is only a part of the human cycle and not an end to it is the joy of faith in the resurrection. However, to be fully conscious, this promise and hope in the promise must coexist with the truth of transitoriness in our lives now.

Mircea Eliade wrote, "Initiation is a passing by way of symbolic death and resurrection from ignorance and immaturity to the spiritual age of an adult."[1] If there is a way to blunt the ravages of transitory time, it is not literal—thing-oriented—but metaphorical and mythic. Initiation into the life of faith means dying to our petty claims to exemption from the conditions of existence in favor of rebirth to a new existence. This new existence is the one animated by the love that lets go of clinging and control. Love is the only and ultimate doorway beyond our mortal limits. To love unconditionally with a full yes to every condition of existence grants safe passage to new life. Such life is accessible in this immediate here and now. If we say that God is love here and now, then the God-life is here when love is here, and it is in the now when love is happening now.

The Book of Wisdom addresses God: "You have arranged all things by measure and number and weight" (11:20). The universe endlessly elaborates itself into the farthest reaches of space. *I am one such elaboration.* In this sense, there is no circumference to reality. Psyche is nature become conscious of itself. Absolute refers to the origin and life force of the ongoing evolutionary cycle. Since the cycle of evolution also includes dissolution, opposites alternate with one another and are united.

Life is thus always happening in two phases: evolution and dissolution. The goal of an adult spirituality is to welcome both sides. Then we are not devastated by the fact of dissolution but trust its phase-appropriateness. To come to the point of being able to say yes to its most terrifying configurations is true fortitude. I am consoled that this is a phase that makes evolution possible, and I can trust myself to live through it. I am also grateful to the assisting forces around and beyond me.

We can also summon images of calm (i.e., grant calm) that reflect our potential to say yes to all the passing show of life and nature no matter how scary it becomes. In order to travel with it, we ride the horse in the direction in which it is going. That ride is called *unconditional yes* to the givens of existence. It is the way we fulfill our human destiny to live gracefully among people and things. We are not here to live as long as we can, but to live long enough to manifest the unconditional love, perennial wisdom, and healing power of a higher power than ego, the indwelling Spirit beyond the fearful self. The human psyche asks why. The universal psyche, the one that includes the Holy Spirit, says yes.

Impermanence also refers to the fact that life is unpredictable. Present positive evidence gives no guarantee of a positive future. Present discouraging evidence does not necessarily presage disaster. The childish response to life's unpredictability is to seek out safe and reliable certitudes. "There will always be a silver lining" is an immature wish meant to buy off the uncontrollable realities of life. It beguiles us away from the unbluntable bluntness of truth. The adult response is simply to allow, to accept what cannot be changed. This is the antidote to wishful thinking.

A lively faith happens in the paradoxical gap that opens in the human mind when confronted with, first, the apparent arbitrariness of nature and history *and*, second, a belief in an upholding and reliable providence. One and two seem irreconcilable, but the combining word *and* closes the gap. Simultaneously, we are held and we are not held; we are both in the grace of circumstance and at the mercy of circumstance.

Nature is unpredictable as it moves toward an omega point of coherence. Faith accommodates a both/and where logic sees only an either/or. Faith never expunges or simplifies our human story. It enriches it by the paradox of simultaneity, the union of opposites.

Providence is often invoked as a *deus ex machina* in the midst of crisis. Actually, providence means that in the face of suffering, cruelty, death, and injustice, we have it in us to go on loving. This is how it "all works out for the best." It is not that external situations rectify themselves but that our powers of love remain intact no matter what happens to us. Our capacity to love survives the pain and abuse we have experienced. That is the meaning of spiritual survival. It is also what is meant by providence as a power that upholds us.

Paul Tillich presented the mature view of providence as the following:

> Faith in divine providence is the faith that nothing can prevent us from fulfilling the ultimate meaning of our existence. Providence does not mean a divine planning by which everything is predetermined....Providence means that there is a creative and saving possibility implied in every situation, which cannot be destroyed by any event. Providence means that the demonic and destructive forces within ourselves and our world can never have an unbreakable grasp upon us, and that the bond which connects us with the fulfilling love can never be disrupted.[2]

PAIN IS PART OF EVERY STORY

To insist that suffering not be a part of life in any way is to say no to a given of existence. That no is the cause of more suffering. Fidelity to ourselves requires that we engage with our own inner struggles long enough to gain their blessing, like Jacob wrestling the angel. We can accept and endure pain and wait for its meaning to reveal itself to us—or not. We can also console ourselves in the midst of it with a belief in its ultimate meaning or in the "silver lining" we hope is within it. "Meaning makes things endurable, perhaps everything," wrote Carl Jung.[3] Is the meaning we find based on imagination or on reality? That is the ultimate question for enlightened-by-faith people. There is indeed a positive dimension to everything when the teaching of Christ can be found in it, and we have not lost our ability to receive it.

The Roman poet, Terence, wrote, "Nothing human is alien from me." As our faith expands, we let go of believing that we are exempted from the bad luck or painful events that other people suffer. There is no "It can't happen to me."

The humility of Christ was precisely in accepting that anything from people or reality that can happen to any human could happen to him. That is what it means to take our place in the human community in Christ. As the Suffering Servant, he is the archetype of how acceptance can redeem pain.

St. Teresa of Avila said that when we accept what happens to us and make the best of it, we are praising God.[4] This is because our yes to what happens is a yes to God's will. "Accept" in this context does not mean resignation to pain but an entrance into it, finding a kernel of value in it, and a release from it. What makes life exhilarating is noticing how we evolve through the events that happen to us, painful and otherwise. What makes life exciting is our commitment to that conscious yes everywhere and in everything. This is an example of the bigness of our faith; we do not see suffering as an unfair burden but as a necessary part of our personal and collective evolution. In fact, all the conditions of existence are the specific *requisites* for becoming people of character, depth, and compassion, as we saw above.

Pain toughens us. An incoherent, fragile, or unstable person could not live out the hero path. It takes a strong ego but not a retaliatory, inflated, or controlling one. Pain provides an impetus toward individuation and a doorway to higher consciousness. We are now in spiritual territory where ego explanations fall short. A higher power, that is, a higher consciousness, God, has to be acknowledged and accessed. The pain that happens to us is pedagogy. It teaches us how to let go of fear and desire, to find our deepest needs, values, and wishes, and to fulfill our destiny. Pain is the price of these opportunities for spiritual progression.

If the suffering we undergo becomes conscious to us, it redeems itself. In fact, redemption in the Christian myth is precisely this: Christ chose to be placed at the mercy of evil *as a spiritual practice* and thereby redeemed the evil done to him. This is why suffering does not have to be an affliction that is imposed on a victim or a penalty imposed on a culprit. John Keats wrote in a letter, "How then are souls to be made? How then are these sparks which are God to have identity given them—so as ever to possess a bliss peculiar to each one's individual existence? How but by the medium of a world like this? . . . Do you not see how necessary a world of pain and troubles is to school an intelligence and make it a Soul? A place where the heart must feel and suffer in a thousand diverse ways!"[5]

Pain has worked for us when it leads to a greater consciousness of our psycho-spiritual identity, a respect for the givens of existence rather than expecting indulgence in the face of them. This means less entitlement to special treatment, more compassion, more humor, more effective relationships, and a sense of belonging, being part of a whole, of living in communal context. In the *Gospel of Thomas*, people dance around Christ who is standing cheerfully in the center.

A cosmic dimension in suffering opens when we experience it for the whole of humanity. We suffer something and thereby know how to help others who suffer it too. Experience does more than teach us; it equips us to become healers. We are all interrelated, so our suffering not only deepens us but enables us to understand and assist others when their pain is similar to our own. This is how pain is a path to compassion, one taken by all the saints. A saint is someone who puts his or her own conviction to live in love above selfish gain or even survival.

Wounds are identification marks, as St. Thomas learned. In the image of his wounded and light-emitting heart, Jesus says, "This is what I am." Jesus found his full identity through his wounds. Our scars present our identity even physically inasmuch as everyone has a different set of them in different places, forming a unique design on the body. The questions are the following: How is this pain connected to the totality of our lives? How does this crisis reveal us to ourselves? What is the loving intent in the universe that makes this a gift?

The *I Ching* says, "It is only when we have the courage to accept things as they are, without any sort of self-deception or illusion, that a light will develop out of events, by which the path to triumph may be recognized." Development happens by affirming responses from our parents and friends throughout life. Inner character develops the same way, through our affirming responses to our predicaments. In fact, the difference between suffering that hinders growth or helps it happen is that neurotic suffering resists the conditions of existence while authentic suffering embraces it.

Resurrection is the archetype of hope; a way of acknowledging that death and evil are not final. We recall this metaphor in Revelation: "The devil has come down to you with great wrath, because he knows that his time is short!" (12:12). This hope animates us. Pentecost—the animation of the disciples by the Holy Spirit—directly results from the resurrection. It is one ongoing and coherent initiation. Pain is the characteristic of any initiatory process. Death and the cross are conditions of transformation not just conditions of existence. That is the good news of redemption. Ovid in his *Fasti VI* stated it too: "There is a god in us who, stirring, kindles us."[6] That god is reality stirring us toward yes.

Finding serenity and resting in its sequestered sanctuary is not the spiritually mature program in the face of pain. Such tranquillity can itself become an object of attachment or a distraction from the path. The reality is beyond peace and conflict in the real refuge of faith that is reality itself as just what we need to know our path.

At the same time, Carl Jung reminds us that "the divine sometimes asks too much of us."[7] Sometimes nothing can be done and we confront "the things that cannot be changed." Hanging on the cross in full consciousness of so many contradictions was Jesus' spiritual practice: "He would not drink [the drugged vinegar]" (Matt 27:34). This is difficult for those taught to do something about anything uncomfortable. Yet a vision of divine meaning happens only after suffering has been endured. Job found this out: "*Now* my eye sees you" (42:5, emphasis added).

WHEN LIFE IS UNFAIR

Every human life will include physical pain, emotional pain, and spiritual pain. A childish response to pain might be that it is punishment, while happiness is a reward. Such beliefs are wishes that reality be fair, that someone or something mete out appropriate rewards and punishments and keep us safe through it all. The mature realization is quite the opposite: suffering is not a penalty; happiness is not a reward.

Notice that "fairness" in this respect may mean a wish to punish those who cross us and is thus contrary to the Sermon on the Mount: "Love your enemies; do good to those who hate you" (Luke 6:27). Jesus did not desire to punish but to transform. We see this option in the following prayer found at the women's concentration camp at Ravensbrück in 1945:

> O God, remember not only the men and women of good will

but also those of ill will.
But do not remember only the suffering they have inflicted on us.
Remember the fruits we bought thanks to this suffering:
our comradeship, our loyalty, our humility, and the courage,
generosity, and greatness of heart that has grown out of all this.
And when they come to judgment let all the fruits
we have borne become their forgiveness.

When we love one another, we do not have ill will against those who are unjust toward us or anyone. We wish their transformation. We let them be and we return love for hate. This is a big-hearted faith response and happens more when we let ourselves feel our pain, say "Ouch!" and attempt to open a dialogue with the person who hurt us. We grieve for the pain we have incurred and for the pain in the one who hated or hurt us. All this is done in a spirit of compassion. The wish to punish is puerile and itself evil. Rehabilitative compassion is the way of Christ and of enlightened masters. Bruce Sanguin, in *Darwin, Divinity, and the Dance of the Cosmos,* wrote that the temptation of Christians is either to minimize evil or to give it ultimate status. Rather, we are called, with Christ, to enter into the suffering of all creation, trusting in God's redeeming power, known in and through the presence of noncoercive love.[8]

Once we say God is love, then the power of God is love, not coercive force. In fact, when power *is* love, there is no room for punishment or retaliation. Justice finds a way to be merciful. To say that God is love is to affirm that love creates, sustains, redeems, and sanctifies the world—the graces of the Trinity. Love is the wholeness we are here to express in our every gesture and choice. The result is a sense of being held and of having the power to hold the world in our hearts. As Mother Teresa said, "I am in Jesus' heart and Jesus is in my heart." Any sense of something missing is transformed into a conviction that everything has been received. For that we have abiding gratitude.

Here is a challenging example of a new perspective. It is understandable to think of Hitler in hell. Is it also possible to break out of the punishment model in favor of the bigness of the restoration model. With cosmic-wide compassion, we can think of him in a strict but restorative monastery with an abbot who keeps reminding him of the suffering he caused and showing him how to repent. Then, gradually he might be ready to ask forgiveness from everyone he hurt. *Hell* and *monastery* are both metaphors, so why not this version of Hitler's fate rather than the coal-shovelling one? Is it not more advantageous to have an abbot instead of a devil in our consciousness? It makes for more love in our own hurt, and at times hurtful, hearts. This is how we contact the bigness of love that wrote these words in our calling to be universal humans: "God is love."

Why does God not intervene in evil and injustice? Why did God not halt the Holocaust or stop a rape or murder? These are questions that expect God to be coercive and cancel human freedom. Divine love impels; it does not compel. Evolution shows the noncoercive and gradual style of creation. Everything real takes time to develop and includes a dark chapter. A life opens to cycles and seasons. A full conception of the Divine will include the elements of the Hindu trinity: creation, destruction, and preservation. All three are permitted and all three have their own timing.

To omit the dark side is to impoverish divine wholeness and to contradict the evidence of nature.

Suffering is an evil in accord with nature's laws. Deliberate malice is an evil that is human-made and deliberately inflicted out of hatred for the victim. The suffering of life is to be expected and handled with care by us and with caring for others. Deliberate evil is to be confronted and fought, never accepted passively or apathetically.

The given of suffering in life includes a given of malice and evil. This is what Carl Jung referred to as the shadow side of ourselves and of society. War, the Holocaust, atomic weapons, international terrorism, and so on, represent the societal given of evil. A personal given is our penchant to be dishonest, hurtful, violent, or malicious at times. We are sometimes the perpetrators of evil. We are the victims of evil not of our own making. Perhaps this is the metaphorical meaning of "original sin."

"Why do the innocent suffer?" This question presupposes that the guilty *should* suffer and the innocent *should* be happy. This is a juvenile wish and not the way the world works. To an adult, indiscriminate pain is not taken personally. It is always a probability. Suffering happens even in the context of the firmest connection to the Divine: "The Father and I are one" (John 10:30), were the words of one cruelly and unjustly betrayed and crucified. The suffering referred to here is an evil, but it is an unplanned evil. It differs from the evil of an injustice that is maliciously planned, chosen, and implemented.

The promise of faith is not that bad things will not happen to good people, but that goodness will survive and that good people can become better through it all.

The challenge of faith is to believe in design despite display. The display is what occurs in our story, what happens. The design is the transcendent reality that underlies all of history, the transcendent dimension in what happens. It synchronously and randomly challenges our capacity to grow through pain. Faith accepts the fact of the givens and the fact that miracles occasionally break through to defy the givens on our behalf. Having faith means having a capacity to love that endures no matter what the impact of the events.

Hurt, hate, and betrayal—though never to be sought—figure in the making of the hero. Joseph could not sell himself into slavery; he had to be betrayed into it by his brothers. Jonah could not jump overboard to meet the whale; he had to be thrown by the ship's crew. Jesus did not turn himself over to the Sanhedrin; he was betrayed to them by Judas. Dorothy could only get from the Kansas of status quo to the Oz of wonder by being tossed there by a tornado. In every one of these archetypes, the hero/heroine progresses toward his or her destiny by being at the effect of an evil. Maybe everyone who ever hurt or disappointed us "threw" us out of our comfortable delusions and helped us find our personal character, strength, and truth.

Emerson says in his "Essay on Experience" that we can all accept "our actual companions and circumstances, however humble or odious, as the mystic officials to whom the universe has delegated its whole pleasure for us."[9] Synchronicity, meaningful coincidence, happens through a series of similar events. A man loses his job, finds out his wife is having an affair, totals his car, and learns he has cancer of the prostate—all in the course of a year. These events are certainly the ingredients for despair when all we have going for us is our egos. However, perhaps there is a loving intent in all that occurs. What if all these things have happened to give us new opportunities for growth?

Perhaps all that happens to us happens so that we can

finally let go of our controlling or arrogant ego and learn to love more. Perhaps crises are meant to give us a push away from a passive or stultifying routine. Perhaps they instill a sense of vulnerability and the need for trust in powers beyond ourselves.

Dreams and images that arise at these straitening and terrifying times often reveal meanings in the crises. The loving intent in what has happened to us is also revealed by what the events make us do. For instance, we have to ask for help now, whereas we were too self-sufficient to do that before. We have become more tender or compassionate, qualities that may have been out of character for us before all this happened.

Synchronous events in life are not just coincidences and bad breaks; they are breakthroughs of the spiritual into our too time-encapsulated lives. Here are some questions that may help us find the depth and meaning of the events in our life story:

"What is the question for which this provides the answer?"
"How can this help me love more?"
"How is this helping me *be* more?"

OUR SENSE OF ALONENESS

Even though I walk through the darkest valley, I fear no evil; for you are with me. —Psalm 23:4

Almost any form of pain can be endured when a companion appears and stays with us as we go through it. In the Christian good news, God not only sent, he came; God not only came, he stayed. *Can we stay with ourselves?*

We live in the community of all humans. At the same time, it is certainly true that each of us lives his or her life as a single person; each is born and dies alone. The neurotic response is to fill our lives with external events, people, and dramas. The adult approach is to appreciate the solitude while still reaching out to others and enjoying their company.

An adult accepts periods of aloneness as important to the process of growth. This is an archetypally feminine feature of the hero's work. Jack was hidden in the cupboard (womb) by the giant's wife before his daring battle. Bellerophon kept vigil in the temple of Athena before fighting the monstrous Chimera. His reward for staying was a magic bridle to tame the Pegasus, given to him by the goddess. In both metaphors, female assistance came to the hero after his willingness to be alone, isolated, and contained. The archetypal and alchemical motif of containment is a crucial piece on the board of transformation. Christ in the womb of Mary is the Christian example of this same period of gestation within the female container before the epiphany occurs. Containment-in-preparation is an optimistic way of reckoning periods of aloneness on our journey.

In the psyche, there is a sense of a protecting presence that ends or cuts through isolation. Again and again in Scripture, there are phrases that offer hope to our aloneness: "I will fear no evil; for you are with me" (Ps 23:4); "Stay with us [Lord], because it is almost evening" (Luke 24:29); "Remember, I am with you always" (Matt 28:20). But sometimes the sense of presence disappears in the face of a terrifying existential absence. Christ felt this on Calvary: "Why have you forsaken me?" He shared in our greatest terror: to feel abandoned, utterly alone. This was the very thing the Scriptures seem to have promised would never happen. But Jesus is the archetype of the redeeming power of accepting the given of aloneness. His share in human forsakenness shows it to be bearable, legitimate, temporary, and redemptive.

Every great mystic felt this aloneness, though each was a person of faith. So faith does not exempt us from this or any given of human existence. Not one given will be repealed, abolished, or annulled just for us. We have no entitlement to special treatment. There are no disclaimers in adulthood. The leap of faith is from the childish belief that religion offers a reliable consoling end to aloneness to the mature belief that aloneness coexists with faith. Childhood's either/or continually gives way to both/and.

In fact, taking refuge in God does not mean finding a refuge from the conditions of existence but becoming a refugee in the midst of them, like our forebear, Jesus, who had "nowhere to lay his head" (Matt 8:20). Often we find no sense of accompaniment when we are in the void of aloneness. The predicament of finding no answer *is* the void. Despair is the void. It has no dimension and that is what is so terrifying about its isolation.

Aloneness can feel like a deep vacancy within us. Then it scares us with a sense of personal emptiness and the absence of any support. Aloneness can also feel like a deep *spaciousness* within us, one that opens onto a vast explorable horizon. Then it is positive and gladdens us with a sense of presence. A consequent sense of an accompanying presence is, in effect, the other side of locating the depth dimension of our own presence. The negative aloneness leads to a sense of loneliness and worthlessness, which we attempt to erase with attachments and addictions. This is our neurotic ego holding onto something that can fix us. The positive aloneness leads to welcome solitude and growth in a sense of inner worth. We are then receptive to what next may bloom. This is our healthy ego not holding on but feeling held. The irony is that we feel held precisely when we no longer hold on. We see this in Psalm 139: "If I take the wings of the morning and settle at the farthest limits of the sea, even there your hand shall lead me, and your right hand shall hold me fast" (vv. 9–10).

Neurotic aloneness with its frantic hunger for distractions is a hole in us. The functional aloneness with its abundance to give is the whole in us. When I ask myself "Who am I?" I quickly answer with a list of characteristics that delineate my roles and choices in life. But this list tells me exactly who I am not. Roles and choices are meant to satisfy my desire to fill myself from the outside and find approval in the bargain.

Aloneness is a useful path to discover who we are: nothing but space for what is here and now and what may be. Giving up the illusion that others make us whole, we gain a sense of wholeness in our solitude. We notice both our spaces and our boundaries. We automatically know how to take care of ourselves. This combination of receptiveness, an unconditional yes to that which is—and self-nurturance in the midst of what is—turns out to be the most adult identity card we carry.

> *What is demanded of a human is not to endure the meaninglessness of life; but rather to bear his incapacity to grasp its unconditional meaningfulness in rational terms.*
> —Viktor Frankl

MEETING DARKNESS IN THE DIVINE

> *There is in God a deep and dazzling darkness.*
> —Henry Vaughn

There is a dark side to any reality. The depth of our psyche is comprised of a union of opposites. This implies that God also contains opposites. God is the eternal light *and* darkness too. The Bible gives many indications of this in story form. The predicament of Job is a prime example of inflicting evil unnecessarily. Other passages in the Old Testament show this: Elijah butchered the priests of Baal. "Does disaster befall a city, unless the LORD has done it?" (Amos 3:6). "The LORD has made everything for its purpose, even the wicked for the day of trouble" (Prov 16:4). "I make weal and create woe" (Isa 45:7). "On the way, at a place where they spent the night, the LORD met him and tried to kill him" (Exod 4:24). "And the LORD said, 'Who will entice Ahab, so that he may go up and fall at Ramoth-gilead?'" (1 Kgs 22:20). These quotations are not to be taken literally. They are ego projections on the Divine by the writers of Scripture. But they do describe how any of us might feel when terrible events befall us and it seems to come from God's dark side.

The words *Lord God* in the Old Testament have come to have an ominous sound because they indicate so much retaliatory—and thereby unforgiving—ego. Yet the Divine is ultimately that which does not give up on us; not that which has to get back at us. When we are like that too, we are disciples of Christ. *Does a cleric stand at the electric chair, Bible in hand, to protest the injustice of capital punishment or as a representative of the system that inflicts it?*

We were taught that God has no shadow but mystics know better. As is so often the case, catechesis may exclude or distort what theology accommodates. Perhaps most of the archetypal truths of religion are consigned to this same sequestered silence. We deny the silence we find in God. We deny the shadow of God perhaps because we deny the magnitude of our own human shadow. We want a God who is our refuge and our strength, a mighty fortress, not an usher to the strict conditions of existence. We fear the refuge of truth and prefer a refuge from it. This is not a reason for shame or a sign of waywardness. It is just what the ego naturally does in its own defense in a world besieged by so much suffering and uncertainty. The challenge is not to forsake any hope of refuge. The challenge is to take refuge where it can be found. It will be in the yes to light *and* shadow. This is just the chiaroscuro world in which we need to evolve as beings of depth, and in it the God of depths grants a lap but not an exemption.

The metaphor of Eden and redemption depicts a God motivated and driven by ego: God shows his shadow before Eve does; he threatens with punishment. He shows it again after the sin when he demands expiation by the death of his Son. The ego God of the Old Testament follows a domination and retaliation model that was later exploited by patriarchal religion to oppose human freedom. Pluralism is an inherent human quality, the vehicle by which we expand and discover the dimensionality of truth. To crush it is to limit our creativity, our godlikeness.

It is true that God is love and that love is tough at times. Storms, earthquakes, the devouring of the weak animals by the stronger ones, and destructive forces unleashed on populations are examples of nature's ruthlessness. Yet this dark side of nature makes evolution possible. The dark side of God is like that of nature; it is an afflicting force that ultimately becomes an assisting one. The inexorable and necessary conditions of existence are the shadow of God. The unity of the Divine, the natural, and the human shows how the shadow of the Self operates in the world. Since the ratio includes nature, it has a destructive dimension as does the Divine, as does the human, as crime and misdeeds attest. The divine collective shadow and the human shadow joined forces for the Holocaust and Hiroshima.

What Carl Jung called the higher Self than ego, God within, is indeed unconditional love, perennial wisdom, and healing power. It is enduringly luminous in those ways. At the same time, the higher Self has a shadow side that can be violent and dangerous: "God is a consuming fire" (Heb 12:29). There is no dualism in the Divine, but there is distinction, light and dark. The dark is not evil, but it is destructive and it is felt as evil by us when we fail to make a full contract with the conditions of existence. The dark side of God is to be revered but not feared. It is how the wholeness of human experience, and of nature, happens. Be not afraid.

> *The Great Mother remains true to her essential, eternal, and mysterious darkness, in which she is the center of the mystery of existence.* —Erich Neumann

DEALING WITH THE CONDITIONS

> *Adult faith is grounded in our commitment to create lovingly alternative responses to every given and condition and our faith is grounded in the hope that this alternative history of life will indeed triumph in the end.* —*Catholic Agitator*, Spring 1991

Mature religion has two contributions to make to our handling of the givens of life: it gives counsel about facing the conditions of existence and points to a meaning in them. We may have believed that religion was supposed to reverse or soften the blows of the conditions of life. When we notice it does not work that way, we may lose our faith. For example, we might claim that if there were a God, he would not have permitted the Holocaust. In courageous faith, we accept the noninterference of the Divine in human choice, the silence of God, the darkness in God.

We also accept that nothing immunizes us to the nature of things. "These are the tears of things,"[10] as Virgil said, landing on reality. We are part of nature and her conditions are ours. Nature accepts and repairs the catastrophes of weather, earth, and sea. Our interior realm of consciousness is the equivalent of space in the far reaches of the cosmos. Equilibrium in nature is the equivalent of equanimity in us. Our challenge is to accept and repair or, if repair is impossible, to accept and move on. The conditions of nature, no matter how distressing, are part of the necessary evolutionary cycle. The givens of our lives, no matter how disturbing, are the building blocks of our virtue and spiritual progress. Hamlet says admiringly of Horatio that he is "A man that Fortune's buffets and rewards. Hast ta'en with equal thanks."[11]

An adult with faith embraces the givens of existence not as heinous flaws in the universe, but as essential facts. We are not victimized by these conditions. They make our life rich and our struggle challenging. The healthy adult honors and acknowledges life's givens with both grief and joy. We grieve the loss inherent in each and rejoice in the manifold variety and surprise of human living. We become really present on earth. The question is not whether God is present but whether we are willing to be.

Without faith, the conditions of existence—transitoriness, pain, unfairness, death, aloneness, divine darkness—are final and life is a cruel joke. With faith, they yield to an ultimate meaning: an immortality behind the appearances of mortality. Big-hearted faith is not an escape from the reality of human conditions, but a realization that they are not the whole picture. They are only the figures that are backed by a ground of spiritual reality, as the ego is supported by the larger life in us called God.

Christian faith looks behind impermanence and suffering to a ground of enduring life. Rotation and alteration express this life, not polarity and dualism. The rhythms of dying and rising are not dichotomies. They imply one another, that is, they exist entirely in mutuality. The resurrection did not cancel death but is implied in death. The mystery is not an empty tomb but a combination of opposites: death and life. Behind it all is the ground of reconciling and healing love enacted by us every time we refuse to give up on love. The risen Christ is the higher aliveness, our true nature, that endures and abides in us.

Faith is tested when we are confronted with apparent contradictions. In Luke 24, the two disciples en route to Emmaus lament that Christ was supposed to set Israel free from the Romans but instead was defeated and his work destroyed. Jesus answers, "Was it not necessary that the Messiah should suffer these things and then enter into his glory?" (Luke 24:26). This response is an assertion of the paradoxical nature of the spiritual vision. The figure of death recedes to ground and the figure of new life emerges from the ground of apparent unalterability. Faith defies the facts at hand. Paradox is the link between the figure we focus on and the ground behind it that we miss. Jesus' apparent defeat is really victory. In the marriage of opposites that characterize faith, one is implied and promised in the other. In the same way, *the disciples' apparent aloneness is really communion with him.* The Everything that they thought was lost is within reach and will break bread with them.

It is spiritually significant that this revelation occurred when the disciples were hopeless. It is often from within the void, the darkness of the Divine, that we hear and see in a new way, another example of how a condition of existence can become a source of new life. Hopelessness, that is, the bankruptcy of the ego's expectations, is actually the condition most suitable to awakening. The reason the void can become so fertile is that it is the very spaciousness that is the ground of all being, the divine essence behind appearances, the space taken by the ego we see through and let go of once we really awaken.

"Your faith has made you well" (Matt 9:22) is a repeated phrase of Jesus that shows how faith has the power to create conditions on earth as they are in heaven. He did not ask for faith in miracles but used miracles as signs of the arrival of a new way of living, one based on big faith. *Miracles are moments in which nature bows to transcendent possibilities.* Bernie Siegel says, "A miracle is an alteration in the direction and flow of creation."[12] A miracle is an inexplicable phenomenon that gives faith more conviction. It is not a proof since proof is in the realm of logic, and faith happens at a higher level of knowing. It is the arrival of something more than the ego thought possible, something that has happened against all odds. It is not that nature's laws do not hold up, but they are suspended to reveal for an instant something that is always the case in the cosmos, a law-transcending power. Miracles invite faith and evoke it, but they do not form the basis of it. They are not proofs but *witnessings* that manifest to faith from faith. They do not produce knowledge but enrich belief.

There are no limits to time and space, so why would grace be limited either? Miracles happen interiorly, for example, inspiration and intuition. They can also happen exteriorly as in healings of the body. Miracles are articulations of grace at work in the world of mind and nature. This grace motivates and assists us, but then we take over with ongoing effort. Grace shows us that the destiny we are headed for is not the ego's making, that wholeness is not owed to us but can always be relied on as a gift to us.

To ask for a God who repeals the conditions of existence for us is to ask for a rescuer, not a higher power. It is to seek exception to what is. However, if *what is* is *God's will*, where is faith in seeking such an exception? Religion negates life when it provides an escape from the givens, a *but* instead of an *and* to each of them. For instance, "I am alone but not really" changes to "I am alone and I trust in a support beyond myself that I may not always feel."

Faith is real when it includes every given with no entitlement to a repeal, and pushes us out to take our chances on involvement with a humanity that grants no guarantees. Christ is the perfect example of this for "though he was in the form of God, did not regard equality with God as something to be exploited" (Phil 2:6).

Why does an adult need spiritually? The child seeks a safe haven from the full gamut of human experience. The adult finds a new center of gravity and a new form of sustenance. "I am the living bread that came down from heaven," Christ announced in John 6:51. The one who touched down on earth to touch and be touched in every human way is the model of personal nurturance. He hovered over every condition of existence and reverently whispered, "This is my body." He was looking at the whole cosmos when he said this. And he said this as the Bridegroom of all that is.

Faith means accepting every condition of human existence, as Christ did. All eventualities become authorized and legitimate. Then we can say, "Yes, it can all happen to me. I am no exception. I accept the best of times and the worst of times, a time to live and a time to die and at the same time, I do—and sometimes fail to do—everything humanly possible to end suffering and injustice."

A big-hearted love of God is love of life's givens as what is good for us. For a child, good is what leads to safety and security, and bad is what does not. As spiritually aware adults, we trust that what challenges us can open us to new possibilities of courage.

To believe is to approach reality with confidence in God as a loving power beyond earthly limits. "A believer interprets reality and human existence as finally worthwhile, intelligible, and purposeful," says Richard McBrien. Faith is a heightened capacity for perceiving what lies behind appearances and the connectedness of it (and us all) with a sense of awe and wonder. From this sense comes ritual and morality. Around it gather beliefs. Thus all of religion composes itself from faith and all faith comes by the graces we find in life's givens.

In the face of life's givens, we then feel not dismay but creative tension between opposites: impermanence and the cycles of death and resurrection. The death can be desolation, but it becomes consolation when new life appears from its ashes. The image of conscious death is that of a ripe apple falling into a mother's lap. We are the apples and earth is our body's mother and the Great Mother of all the living and dying is our heavenly one.

There are two thrusts in the spiritual journey: the desire to escape from mortality while honoring and benefiting from it, and the desire to contact immortality within and beyond ourselves. Union with God is the theological term for wholeness, the combining of mortal and immortal in oneself and in the nature of things. Since the divine life of the psyche/universe works in unfathomable and alogical ways, union with God turns out to be an assent to those natural ways, that is, to the conditions of existence. An unconditional yes to these givens is a powerful form of reverence.

Consent to the orderly plan is oneness with *what is*, another way of saying yes to the "divine will." To say yes to what is makes us one with God; we become the immovable ground and expanding space beneath the conditions and contingencies of existence—a cosmic purpose indeed. Our yes is our transportation to transcendence when it means not just accepting the conditions of existence but being thankful for them and cooperating with them. This is how "all things work together for good" (Rom 8:28).

Perhaps this chapter ends best with a question: What if we were meant to learn as much from pain as we do from joy, as much from crisis as we do from serenity, and as much from loss as we do from love?

> *The hero gives up completely all attachment to his personal limitations, idiosyncrasies, hopes and fears, no longer resists the self-annihilation that is prerequisite to rebirth in the realization of truth....His personal ambitions being totally dissolved, he...willingly relaxes into whatever may come to pass in him....The Law of life lives in him with his unreserved consent.*
>
> —Joseph Campbell

MINDFULNESS AND THE GIVENS OF LIFE

Eastern and Western monasticism gave us a tool for embracing the conditions of existence. Mindful contemplation leads to awakening. This form of prayer happens when we sit meditatively aware of our breathing, no longer under the influence of our thoughts and judgments. We let go of the need to attach ourselves to our story or its outcome. We stay with our breath rather than be suffocated by fear, clinging, shame, control, or the need to change or fix things. Letting go of ego is the result of just such continual witnessing of impermenance.

Serenity in any circumstance may be a gift/result (but not the purpose) of meditation and prayer. Mindfulness meditation or centering prayer alone cannot provide that. Meditation and prayer can reveal our unconscious fears and wishes, and can free us from them. This is how meditation and prayer assist and supplement our psychological work.

Meditation evokes unconscious material into consciousness. That awareness then loosens the hold that same material had on us. This is how it is liberating. It seems that therapy and religious practices are necessary adjuncts to meditation and vice versa. We go to therapy because religion does not have all the answers. We are religious because therapy doesn't either.

Mindfulness meditation, befriending our shadow side, therapy, and religious rituals coordinate a response to pain that frees us from the ego layers and reveals the pearl in the oyster. Milton, in Book VII of *Paradise Lost,* refers to this as the "orient light exhaling first from darkness." Pain itself is never so bad as the layers of self-blame, shame, fear, and so on, that we add to it. Our imagined layers of interpretations and translations, mostly shame based or fear based, make pain more difficult than it might be in itself. The problem is the gap between what is and how we see it, need it to be, or regret it having been. The ego layers also hide the kernel of value in pain, and so we lose both coming and going.

Thomas Merton discovered the value of Buddhist mindfulness practice in contemplation. The human potential movement and Eastern religions have added to the cornucopia of prayer techniques. They have provided valuable insights into the nature of prayer. It is not a way of changing or controlling or fixing things. It is a way of saying yes to what is. It is also a way of asking for what we need. It is not a demand with "must have" energy. It is a serene abiding in what is, with a willingness to let it be.

In mindful awareness, the givens are revealed not as obstacles but as vehicles. A personal experience of loss, for instance, is precisely the encounter with transitoriness that can become the first step toward enlightened faith. Once we appreciate that impermanence is the only reliable reality, we recognize the conditions of existence as Christ's path, how we become his companions, and how we join in his redemptive work. Then the experience of transitoriness *is* the realization of our highest grace in being human: "it is no longer I who live, but it is Christ who lives in me" (Gal 2:20). Christ lives as risen, beyond the cycles of time and space, life and death, and holds them all for us as we go through them. He does not end the pain, only accompanies us in it.

In fact, divine omnipotence is not "the ability to do or undo anything." Divine power is really a transcendent capacity to love. God is not able to end suffering because God built that in as a given of life and even joined us in saying yes to the limits and conditions that ultimately help us grow.

Life and death, growth and decay, activity and rest are not irreconciliably opposing forces but interconnecting and interacting ingredients of the human story. Mindfulness meditation is a direct gaze at the pure and unadorned reality of life with its givens of change and enduring. Nature is both transient *and* cyclical. This means that we can despair and feel hope. We can see desolation and believe in restoration. This is how mindfulness contributes to faith. There is a direct proportion between commitment to meditation and growth in compassion. This is how it contributes to love.

> *It is a law of the universe that retaliation, hatred, and revenge only continue the cycle and never stop it. Reconciliation does not mean that we surrender rights and conditions, but rather that we use love in our negotiations. It means that we see ourselves in the opponent—for what is the opponent but a being in ignorance, and we ourselves are also ignorant of many things. Therefore, only loving-kindness and right mindfulness can free us.*
>
> —Venerable Ghosananda Buddhist Patriarch of Cambodia, "The Human Family," in Donald Mitchell and James Wiseman, *The Spiritual Life*

CHAPTER FOUR

Rediscovering Familiar Religious Themes

The reason that religious symbols became lost is not primarily scientific criticism....The first step toward the non-religion of the Western world was made by religion itself. When it defended its great system, not as symbols, but as literal stories, it had already lost the battle. In doing so the theologians and lay people helped to transfer the powerful expressions of the dimension of depth into objects or happenings on the horizontal plane. There the symbols lose their power and meaning, and become an easy prey to physical, biological, and historical attack.

—Paul Tillich, "The Lost Dimension of Religion," in *Saturday Evening Post*, June 1958

We can appreciate the archetypal wealth perennially present in traditional beliefs. For instance, the need for a purification ritual is common in all religions. The ego always needs to be purified of its arrogance and ill will. Sprinkling water on the heads of the faithful was performed each afternoon in the temple of Isis at Pompeii in Christian times. The Nile was thought to be inhabited by Osiris and washing in it was a rite of purification. This is true even now of the Ganges. Water is universally associated with cleansing. Baptism is a cleansing and a drowning of ego so that it can be reborn in and as the higher Self: God within, Christ consciousness, indwelling Spirit. This is the core belief living in the archetype of purification. Thus, a universal truth underlies the sacrament of baptism. Every faith belief and ritual has just such a core.

The stories in each religion hold pieces of the archetype of the Savior, who shows humanity the path to spiritual awakening. Christianity seems to be unique in that it presents a complete version of the archetype of salvation: a world is waiting for a savior, the arrival of a divine child, who immediately encounters danger but survives; grows to maturity with a sense of calling; faces the dark side; is initiated into a public life of teaching, healing, and presenting a new way of living; meets up with opposition; suffers; dies; rises; ascends yet remains; and sends a Holy Spirit to continue his work and presence through enlightened wisdom and sacraments that enact his saving powers. This all happens because the Savior is more than a teacher; he is the divine, abiding, empowering, accompanying Presence who has joined heaven and earth.

RITUALS AND SACRAMENTS

Rituals acknowledge, enact, and establish the triune ratio of the natural, the Divine, and the human. In other words, they join the things of nature with human words and gestures in honor of the transcendent. Rituals create the consciousness they represent. We can come to them without full faith and increase our faith engendered by our participation in them. Rituals supply and support us in our move toward wholeness.

Regarding rituals, Bernard Lee writes,

> A religious view looks for the meaning of everyday reality by looking beyond what is given to a more all-encompassing reality. Through ritual a total person is engulfed and transported into another mode of existence. In ritual the world as lived and the world as imagined fuse, thereby providing a transformation in one's sense of reality. Thus it is out of the context of concrete acts of religious observance that religious convictions emerge. Ritual is the means for providing the conviction that religious concepts are true; it also makes the culture's ethos reasonable and makes sense of unwelcome contradictions in life. Rituals are symbolic actions expressive of the community's symbolic narratives or sacred stories. These expressions move toward interpreting and understanding the meaning and nature of life, and within our rituals the common life of the community is acted out in the context of remembering, "re-presenting," and anticipating its memory and vision. Our rites are at the center of human life, binding past, present, and future together. Without meaningful and purposeful rituals daily life cannot be made or kept fully human.[1]

In the Diamond Sutra, Buddha compares the teachings, rituals, and images of faith to a raft that is used to get us to the other side of a river. Once we have arrived at the more advanced place, we leave the raft behind and continue our journey on foot. To carry the raft with us would slow us down. A spiritual consciousness includes this sense of the temporariness and the disposability of the means that lead us to the end. St. Thomas, in one of his hymns to the Eucharist, likewise looks to the time when earthly images and mortal forms will yield to the awesome reality beyond forms. Then the veil over the tabernacle falls and we are with Jacob in the house of God at the gate of heaven. This is the same idea.

Religion includes rituals that celebrate passages along the journey of life. All the rituals and practices of religion are means of accessing love, wisdom, and healing. This is how they are valuable. *Sacrament* is from the Latin word for *mysterion*, a Greek word that means "initiation." As I have noted, every human passage to higher consciousness is an initiation into the world beyond ego. Initiation is an encounter with the conditions of existence and a rite of passage through them. They do not yield; we do.

The sacraments of the Church are meaningful since they occur at milestones on our human journey. They are celebrations of passages that are powerful and transformative. In this sense, they produce what they signify. They happen in community, like all passages, and so are witnessed by others. Attention to saints and ancestors who made these passages before us can add meaning to our sense of our spiritual roots.

Sacraments show the grace-bearing power of nature: bread, wine, oil, incense, fire, water, wax, and so on. In this sense, they connect us to the earth, the place where grace so abundantly happens.

As we grow in faith, we realize that sacraments do not have to be limited to traditional forms since divine life infinitely disperses itself in unlimited ways. As adults with spiritual consciousness, we may use the things of nature to design more means of grace than the seven sacraments the Church offers. In fact, the tradition of sacramentals has always encouraged us to do this. Sacramentals are objects and rituals that help us find grace. The heroic journey archetype includes sacramentals in the form of altars, amulets, and talismans. Catholicism has maintained these in its tradition. Altars are associated with Mass, but we can create altars at home or in our gardens. An altar may be a personal shrine that honors what is meaningful in our life and is a place of stability and refuge in daily conflicts. An amulet is a medal with an inscription that we wear to maintain a sense of accompaniment by assisting spiritual forces. It reminds us that we are not alone in the world of ego but partake in a kingdom beyond it. An amulet draws the forces of the cosmos to its wearer who becomes the center of them. This sense of centeredness is what establishes our connectedness. A talisman is an active and transforming object, such as a rosary, that offers a sense of protection.

We can create our own sacramentals and discover access to grace in nature. The creative challenge to us is to design altars, talismans, amulets, and so on, with natural objects, exalted and lowly. Huston Smith suggests that we "think of the links of the great Chain [of Being] as gradations in degree to which matter hosts Spirit and becomes translucent to it." In addition, we can carry or honor cherished family heirlooms such as jewelry that have spiritual resonance for us. This is a way of having recourse to the communion of saints, our ancestors in the faith. None of this has to become magic, but any of it can be miraculous.

The divine life configures itself differently in each unique personality. We each carry a different image of the Divine, as icons depict Christ differently, yet Christ is the same. We each have our unique ways of contacting the numinous. Brother Lawrence found God in the clutter of the kitchen; Moses found God in a cloud. Anything we experience can grip us with divine fervor. This is why religion cannot be narrow nor rituals be limited. To be transformed by any numinous experience is a religious conversion. This includes dreams, synchronicity, predicaments, symptoms, crises, relationships, heroics, the void, visions, responses to nature, and any other experience that grips us with a force that outstrips the ego's powers. To make sincere amends in a twelve-step program is an experience of grace like making a confession.

Nature is meant to be part of healing in therapy and a means of grace in religion. This must be how astrology, crystals, plants, totem animals, and so forth, became so important in the evolution of religion. What herbs are to medicine, nature is to religion. St. Francis is the exemplar of the truly religious man since he found the Divine in the material world. The mystery of the incarnation is that God needs a tabernacle that is time long and space wide, and we humans are limited enough to become it.

> *Sacraments concretely symbolize what they abstractly stand for only when in the course of their performance they make what they represent experientially and personally present in sacred space and time.* —Joseph Martos, *Doors to the Sacred*

WHERE PRAYER WORKS

There are two basic descriptions of how God is real. The conventional theistic view is the one that puts the accent on transcendence. In this view, God is a Supreme Being/Person in heaven who gave us life and can be asked to intervene in our lives. Indeed, our word *God* is from the German *guth* or *gott*, which derives from a Slavonic word meaning "what is invoked." Prayer is our invocation for intervention. Then it seems that God intervenes in some instances and not in others, and for some people but not for others.

In another view, the accent is on immanence. God is within us and we are within God. Here God is the more of whom we are and what nature is, the deeper reality of our personal selves, an inner light that cannot fail. In this view, God is not a person, but an abiding transpersonal presence. This means God is not limited to any one set of personal characteristics. This God is not thought so much to intervene as to be present in every reality and event, and in any case, always grace-giving.

Prayer in this context is thanks for graces and asking for the wisdom to notice and make good use of the graces. Each grace reveals a meaning in our experiences and longings. Brother David Steindl-Rast adds, "If what is called 'God' means, in the language of experience, the ultimate Source of Meaning, then those moments that quench the thirst of the heart are moments of prayer."[2]

Prayer has bad press among the humanists. It seems to represent dualism, an address to a God-out-there. It is also suspect when it seems to serve the ego by petitioning for fulfillments of desires and maintenance of attachments. It can seem superstitious and magical when it asks for a repeal of the conditions of existence. Then it is the ego's entitlement at work. How can we appreciate prayer as a sincere and useful tool for spirituality? How can it be a creative way to articulate the incarnation of divinity in our homespun life?

Prayer can take many directions. Three words help us find our direction: *yes, please,* and *thanks.* These are the prayers of assent, intention, and thanksgiving.

The unconditional yes to the conditions of existence is the prayer of *assent.* We adopt this form of prayer when we accept the reality of our predicament and honor it as a path. Something happens that we cannot fix, change, or stop. We acknowledge ourselves as facing destiny and we surrender to its stern reality. That is the prayer of assent and, like all prayer, it requires no words. It is simply a reverence for reality itself as a transpersonal will with a meaning yet to be revealed. Examples of this prayer in words are the following: "I accept the things that I cannot change"; "I say yes to my here and now situation and to all that will come of it"; and "I let go of having to understand this and let it be."

When we want something to happen for ourselves or others, we can place a firm *intention* for it. It is a spiritual enterprise when it has unconditional love, perennial wisdom, and healing power as its purpose. It is ego-driven—and therefore not prayer—when it has self-aggrandizement, greed, or vindictiveness as its purpose. Here are examples of the prayer of intention: "I change the things that can be changed"; "May I have the wisdom to know the difference between what can and cannot be changed"; "May I become more loving toward those I dislike"; and "May all beings benefit from my spiritual practices."

The prayer of *thanksgiving* is an acknowledgment of the powers of God within, Christ consciousness, indwelling

Spirit. It is a form of praise and appreciation for the gifts of grace. This sense of gratitude is prayer. It can be expressed verbally as "For all that has been: thanks"; "I am thankful for all I have and for all I can give"; and "I am thankful for all the good things that have resulted from my life's sufferings and crises."

All three directions of prayer can be expressed by affirmations, verbally or silently. They can also be forms of meditation. Mindfulness meditation, as I noted earlier, is a powerful way to sit in the center of all three directions of prayer. By sitting and paying attention to our breathing, we let go of the ego's chatter of fear and desire. We become fair and alert witnesses of the passing show of our daily dramas. A shift occurs from identifying with what happens to simply attending to it. We thereby say yes to the reality of ourselves as liberated from the dualism that ego is so adept at creating. We relate to our experience rather than become possessed by it. We enter the silent gap between our struggles and let go of judgment, fear, desire, the need to fix or control, and attachment to an outcome.

In this silent spaciousness—our true nature—a clarity and serenity can open. It then becomes easier to say yes and please and thanks. Such mindfulness in daily situations fulfills St. Paul's suggestion that we "pray without ceasing" (1 Thess 5:17).

Here are some declarations of spiritual wholeness as affirmations.

- I am always opening myself to more consciousness, that is, more light. I notice what I am up to, what my agenda is, where my potential is, and where grace awaits or calls.

- Sometimes I fall down in my resolve to love generously. I admit this without despair. I accept myself as I am, neither condoning all I have done nor castigating myself. I make amends to those I have hurt. I accept responsibility for the consequences I have caused.
- I create an atmosphere of forgiveness and mendable failures in all my relationships. No one is perfect and no one is permanently excluded from my circle of love. I am never at ease as long as I have even one grudge.
- I see that the armor that was protecting me from fear was actually preventing me from being fully free of it. I admit my fears, feel them fully, so they are not able to stop me, and find an alternative that frees me from them. With this program, I am combining defenselessness and resourcefulness.
- I realize that acknowledging a higher power does not excuse me from even one of the conditions of ordinary existence but may grant me more resilience, optimism, and resources in facing them. I acknowledge that spirituality is like an immune system: it does not prevent sickness, but it does make for faster recovery and sometimes less future susceptibility.
- I trust that I have a unique and significant destiny and that everything that happens to me is part of its unfolding. Synchronous events and meetings keep happening for just that reason.
- My destiny is to reach mystical union through a healthy personality and an evolved spirituality. My destiny is thus a holy communion of the human, the natural, and the Divine. I make a fervent

commitment to love wisely and to shower healing upon my world.
- Grace is the life force that energizes my spiritual potential. This force is the same in me, in nature, and in God.

The deepest prayer is yes. This involves letting go of ego. Both egoless spirituality and egoless relationships require what in Greek is called *kenosis*, "an emptying, an exinanition." Christ is the model. In theology, this refers to Christ's emptying himself of divine raiment to become human. In Christian spirituality, *kenosis* is the surrendering of one's own will to the will of God. "Will" in the spiritual context is willfulness, the hubris that puts us first at the expense of what God asks of us, our reckless abandon to creating a world of justice, peace, and love. In religious terms, this selflessness fulfills us because it is the prayer of yes: "Your will be done."

The "yes" attitude of surrender that lets go of the grasping ego allows our inner wholeness, the true center of our identity, God within us, to make a personal appearance. This makes prayer less a statement to someone far from us. It is instead a staying in and with divine presence. We enter the spacious silence within our hearts where Jesus lives. To pray is to speak with his voice, to see with his eyes, to love with his heart. It is a continuous responsiveness to the Holy Spirit that groans with all the universe for the fulfillment of its destiny. To join that energy with ours is the prayer that grants a vision of existence that is no longer vectored by limits of any kind.

In this prayerful open space, we come to understand Christian—and trinitarian—spirituality as a meeting of three challenges and practices:

- To live the life of Jesus in the world by our commitment to his gospel teaching, especially in the Sermon on the Mount. This is our bond with Christ.
- To say yes to all that happens to us as a grace that gives us opportunities to show love. For this we show continual gratitude to the Holy Spirit.
- To remain aware of the abiding presence of God, the Good Shepherd, in our lives: "I will fear no evil, for you are with me." This is our kinship to the Father.

My greatest weapon is silent prayer. —Gandhi

THE CROSS

"For God so loved the world that he gave his only Son." The Son, in this wider metaphysical context, is no longer the one who bails us out or rescues us from our fallen state but the one who becomes our bridge between the realms.

—Cynthia Bourgeault, *The Wisdom Jesus*

Most of us are familiar with the traditional fall/redemption paradigm of the Middle Ages. Matthew Fox has presented a model that more cogently describes how divine love works. The new emphasis in his creation spirituality has been on cosmic salvation and not simply on personal reward.

In the traditional view of redemption, it is accomplished once and for all by Jesus on the cross. He offered himself as the necessary ransom for the outrage of Adam's sin in the Garden of Eden. By virtue of baptism, we are sharers in the forgiveness that resulted from his death. This sharing of grace, however, does not remove the deep flaw that remains in us as a consequence of original sin. This is one of the main reasons we are in need of conservator/father figures who alone have the special charism to rescue us from our ignorance. Left to ourselves, we might sully the integral deposit of faith or never find it. In the conservative perspective, we remain children that always require paternal supervision. There is a direct relationship between many traditional beliefs and the patriarchal Church structure. One supports the other.

The redemption theology begins with sin. Death, suffering, and the other givens of existence are the wages of sin. In the new paradigm, the life energy of the universe is also our life energy. This energy is displayed and *nurtured* by the givens of existence and our response to them. In this context, suffering is part of how life evolves and death is how life transitions to a new mode of being.

In the traditional redemption theology, there is little emphasis on the cosmic Christ who loves the human/divine milieu, where humans err and then are transformed. In the old view, the human being is a sinner, not a powerful steward of the universe. His eternal life comes after death, after suffering, after falling and being forgiven. Is there room in our hearts for the wonderful news that eternal life is happening here and now? The cross is a significant fact of any human journey, but so is the new life of resurrection and Pentecost, in both of which we are invited to co-create a new world.

Sinners who are weighed down by guilt are not usually oriented toward co-creating a world of justice, peace, and love. The ascetic life may not contain an attitude of joy. Mortification brings dualism into the spiritual life.

Asceticism and the choice for pain is not the path that helps us grow. The healthy alternative is a commitment to self-discipline in the fulfillment of a goal.

Many people in history became saints under the most life-denying and self-negating conditions. They interpreted the cross as an invitation to unhealthy ascetic practices. Whatever benefit resulted was not because of those actions but in spite of them. When faith becomes big enough to honor human health, we no longer seek or absorb suffering. We no longer want to hurt ourselves or let ourselves be hurt. The old phrase *offer it up* is self-negating, that is, inner life-negating, God-negating. It recommends powerlessness, nonassertiveness, and absorption of pain. True spirituality is not possible with that kind of psychological dysfunctionality. The only pain to be accepted and offered is that which has not responded to our attempts to relieve it. Always, health in spirituality builds on psychological health.

Indeed, St. Thomas said that "grace perfects nature." John Milton, in *Pardise Lost*, adds, "God and nature bid the same."[3] To be an adult means no longer seeing the "will of God" as an excuse for holding onto pain or for sitting back instead of sitting up at attention. Edward Schillebeeckx says, "The will of God means blasphemy when it is the absolutizing of the status quo, of blind change, or of one's own view projected onto God."[4] For an adult who has spiritual consciousness, "the will of God" simply means "what is" either after any attempts to change it have failed or after our efforts have succeeded in changing it. The final arrangement, the unalterable result, the redemption that happens beyond our human powers, the pain beyond our control: all represent dimensions of what is and that can be called the will of God.

Underlying the redemption/fall approach is a suspicion

about and an impugning of the human body. St. Augustine regards the body and the soul in conflict. Meister Eckhart, on the other hand, believes that the soul loves the body. These two traditions have always existed in the Church, but in our childhood, we may have known only the life-denying one. In our present adult life of big faith, cosmic consciousness, we are hearing the life-affirming side and it matches what we always carried deep within our psyches as the truth.

Some religious artists around the world have transformed the geometry of the cross into a new image, one more in line with resurrection than death. It is the statue of Jesus with his arms outstretched, as if to say, "Come and follow me." It is also a gesture that friends and family make when they want to hug someone, so Jesus is also saying, "You are my beloved friend; I will hold you forever in my infinite arms." These forms also seem to express a feeling of "I have no enemies, and I invite you to join your heart with mine and also have no enemies." These statues, often outdoors in nature, express some of that vision. They are a healthy alternative to so much focus on the crucifix.

In the mystery of the cross and resurrection, love seems overcome by evil but then overcomes it. The powers of greed, hate, and injustice sent Jesus to the cross. Yet later the Christian community saw that it was for the best since that event presented a model for our life purpose: to fight the powers of domination and to trust that even if we die in the process, a new life will come to us and through us to all humanity—the unconditional object of our love in life and death. We go from cross to arms outstretched.

Christ's cross is a metaphor for carrying the pain that is a given in our life journey. We can learn from Jesus' example and open to his grace. We can carry the events of our lives differently from the way our ego would: If others hurt us we do not hurt back. If our suffering requires a journey to Calvary, we take that path. We join Jesus in carrying our cross *redemptively*. This means opening to what can't be changed, bearing it with courage, and growing spiritually from it. This is the Christian alternative to acting destructively toward oneself or vindictively toward others. However, we do not choose or tolerate unwarranted pain that can be avoided; rather we embrace the pain that is inherent in daily life.

The Stations of the Cross, familiar from our childhood, provide an example. They may at first seem maudlin or inordinately focused on the gruesome details of Christ's sufferings. However, as a metaphor, they walk us through the steps of the letting go of our ego. They detail how ego has to accept the weight of the world's unfairness, how it finds few people willing to join in bearing it, how it is leads to full self-denudation, how it has to hang suspended and helpless, and how it has to be buried and lie in silence. These are stations, but we can't forget they are aimed at and are the way to resurrection. Look how the wisdom of the ages was always right there around us in the church, waiting to be acknowledged in its depth dimension! To do that is to open our arms so they reach from east to west and all galaxies between. We can hear this speech from Shakespeare's *Troilus and Cressida* as words of the suffering Christ:

> Time, force, and death,
> Do to this body what extremes you can;
> But the strong base and building of my love
> Is as the very center of the earth,
> Drawing all things to it.[5]

THE EUCHARIST

The Church has beautifully preserved the secret of our true identity as humans in the teaching on the Eucharist. St. Thomas wrote in his hymn *Adoro Te Devote,*

I adore you, concealed divinity,
It is you who are veiled under these appearances.

That applies to the Eucharist, but also to all living things, including us. Under the appearances of our human flesh and blood is our true but hidden identity, divine life, God. In a cosmic perspective, we too are sacraments, like the Eucharist, outward tangible signs of an inner divine reality. This liberating realization is true eucharistic faith. We have finally placed the Eucharist in the monstrance of the universe that deserves perpetual adoration.

Many of us have cherished the Eucharist all our lives. Perhaps part of that loyalty was awareness that it was a key to finding our own identity. Carl Jung wrote, "This life is the way to the long sought-after path to the unfathomable which we call divine....Give me your hand, my almost-forgotten soul."[6]

The emphasis over the centuries on how the Eucharist was really God himself was a long-standing preservation of the wonderful fact that God is the essence, the "substance," the "real presence" of us and of the world too. The theology of the Eucharist securely held that message for two thousand years, and now—thanks to Pierre Teilhard de Chardin, Carl Jung, and the new cosmology—we can open it fully and see its rich and long-hidden meaning. It is the full description of us and of all of nature. It is as extensive as the incarnation itself, embracing all of matter, and is one with the Spirit.

Above all, the Eucharist is also the living archetype of spiritual nurturance, "the true bread from heaven" (John 6:32). Bread is earthly and finite. Something mortal becomes immortal sustenance. This is a way of referring to our own identity and our own destiny, earthbound and yet having a transearthly origin and end.

Bread and wine are fruits of nature. The natural is to the human as it is to the Divine. The Eucharist is a uniquely powerful and touching way to articulate the triune ratio.

The Eucharist is likewise that which continually nourishes us on our faith journey. This is the meal of the believing community that sustains and develops it. From the alchemical point of view, it is the greatest representation of the mystery of transformation: the least valued nutritionless thing is really the most valuable, all-nourishing thing. This reverse of the ordinary is visible only to those who have learned to see in a new way: that which to anyone else is worthless, is to someone who has been initiated, the most cherished of all realities.

We have used the word *thing* above, but the reality is that the Eucharist is a verb referring to a living experience. Jean-Luc Marion, in *God Without Being*, points out that the real presence can turn out to be about "thingness" rather than about the love and communion generated by the act of Eucharist. He refers to this as "prismatic" rather than limited. The concluding Latin words addressed to the people in the Mass of the Roman Rite, *Ite, Missa est*, can be translated: "Go forth to live this Mass in the world." The experience at Mass sends out prismatic love in all directions. We are its light-bearers, emissaries to the entire cosmos. Christ gathered disciples and then sent them to spread his good news. The Eucharist is not complete when it is a gathering; it has to be a sending too: *Ite, Missa est.*

The Mass is a community event that provides an emblem for the divine life that has become really present in us, for us, and with us. It is the archetype of nourishment, the viaticum on the journey to individuation and spiritual wholeness. It is to be eaten as a life-giving food, an assisting force of strength-giving power on our path. Through it, Christ is present as an intimate partner and so it is a form of union. As St. Bonaventure says, "We seek God as the Spouse not the teacher."[7]

There is indeed an intimacy in religion because it shows the union of mortal and immortal. This intimacy appears particularly in the Eucharist since the granting of it and the farewell of Jesus happened at the same supper. The Eucharist is a nourishing way Jesus found to stay with us. Why else does he give it to us on his last night on earth? It is the supremely sensitive gift of a "tremendous lover" of humankind. He knew what it meant to feel bereft, and he addressed and healed that in the gift of his ongoing presence in the Eucharist, the end of aloneness.

Presence in a sustaining way is the deepest meaning of compassion. Compassion is accompaniment. St. Augustine says, in a sermon on the Eucharist, "The body of Christ gives the body of Christ to the body of Christ." The presence is in all of us in our uniquely diverse ways. The real presence in the Eucharist refers to an access to God through the mutual celebration of Mass. Since the deepest reality of human beings is divine, anytime someone is really present to us, we are in the presence of the Divine. Likewise, the whole cosmos is the exposition of the Blessed Sacrament.

The Eucharist indeed represents the transparence of all matter: something behind appearances is personal and loves us. Bread becomes the power that captures and mediates the love in the universe, that which moves and motivates evolution. The Mass speaks directly to the impermanence of the world since it is always anchoring us. It is *this*, the same no matter what is happening in the changing tides.

Carl Jung saw the Mass as the supreme rite of individuation since it has to do with the discovery of human wholeness. The Mass does not repeat a past event but reveals an ever living event: the passover of Jesus from death to life and all of us along with him. The liturgy is not a repetition of the Last Supper but a renewal of its promise of divine life in us. What is that life? It is love of all people and nature, respect for inner wisdom, and ongoing incarnation in the world of our evolving spiritual consciousness. "Inner" after all, also means within a human bond, the realm between humans.

The Mass is the most elegant and deeply religious rite ever devised. It has endured because it combines the four elements of religion—belief, morality, ritual, and devotion—with the three elements of the divine Self—love, wisdom, healing—in the context of the triune equation—cosmos, divinity, and humanity. Everything comes together; everything is now in reach. We see the cosmic significance of Eucharist in this glowing mystical realization of Pierre Teilhard de Chardin:

> I begin to understand: under the sacramental species....the arms and the heart which you open to me are nothing less than all the united powers of the world which, permeated through and through by your will, your inclinations, your temperament, bend over my being to form it and feed it and draw it into the blazing center of your infinite fire. In the host, Lord Jesus, you offer me my life.[8]

THE SACRED HEART

Heart of Jesus, heart of evolution, unite me to yourself. —Pierre Teilhard de Chardin[9]

The Constitutions of the Religious of the Sacred Heart states,

> We are convinced that the love of Jesus can be made known through us and can transform selfishness into love and concern. This conviction is for us a source of joy....In all the circumstances of our life, wherever our mission leads us, our sole purpose in living is to glorify the Heart of Jesus, to discover and make known His Love.... We are sent by the Church to communicate the love of the Heart of Jesus.

As we noted earlier, a stunning symbol of the bigness of our spiritual heritage is the Sacred Heart of Jesus.[10] It demonstrates that God wants to love us with a human heart. It shows that a human heart is big enough to love all humanity. It shows how God is love. Indeed, there are some ways of loving that God can only show us as a fellow human.

By exposing his heart, Jesus reveals that his interior life is accessible and shareable, "the boundless riches of Christ" (Eph 3:8). The image of Christ's heart is also an externalizing of the possibilities of unconditional love in us. The heart of Jesus with its unending and all-embracing love is indeed the template of every human heart. That image of divine actuality reflects our human potentiality. We already have the love that can free us from ego-fear. It is just a matter of noticing it, of seeing it, and of showing it. As we let go of ego—a painful, scary process—we radiate the love that makes our hearts like that of Jesus: open, vulnerable, and giving.

The Sacred Heart is a living symbol. A symbol is another Real Presence. A sign and what it signifies are separate. A symbol is distinct from the reality it represents but not separate from it. Thus, the human body is a symbol of the human person, the self-presentation of the soul. The body is the bodiliness of a spiritual presence. All beings are thus symbolic, because they have to express themselves to be themselves, precisely the nature of a symbol. Symbols proclaim, reveal, express, and concretize reality. The sacraments are the symbols of the central sacrament, the Church.

True devotion happens when we see Christ's heart as the mirror of and call to our own destiny of love. The heart is the core of our lively energy and wholeness. Jesus' heart affirms the deepest core of the universe and of God. It is the symbol of an unconditional gift of himself that Jesus makes to us. The supreme lively energy of all the universe and time thus enters the body/mind of our limitations. The heart is the point of meeting of spirit and matter.

The heart of Jesus is the reality of the convergence of opposites that characterize the spiritual journey. The pierced heart entirely open, always giving, fully committed, unfailingly loving whether or not we love in return. As Karl Rahner wrote, "Since Christ does not release us from his fate, let us hope that we will discover in our association with the sacrament of his Heart what we will be and what we really are."[11]

The Sacred Heart has a long-standing devotion in the Church. It was made popular in recent centuries because of the visions of St. Margaret Mary in the seventeenth century. In the context of her time, the promises of the Sacred

Heart made sense. Today the ones that are not biblically rooted may seem superstitious. We can distinguish the divine origin of a vision from subjective elements in the visionary: personality, historical context, and influences on the visionary. All these affect the content of the message that has to be rethought for today's world. A devotion to the heart of Jesus appealing to modern people is yet to appear in the Church. That is a true loss of the passionate spirituality of devotion, which is an essential feature of the religious instinct.

The central point of a renewed devotion to the Sacred Heart is challenge and capacity, not promises. It is a call to love without reserve. Once we say that God is not one being among others, we can only love God by loving others. The urgency to elicit from our hearts the fullness of love is the essence of the devotion to the Sacred Heart. In fact, devotion empowers us to do it. Everyone of us can contribute to new paradigms that enliven and renew something that so touchingly represents the integration of personal love and spiritual evolution.

The revelations of the Sacred Heart to St. Margaret Mary are certainly a turning point in the history of our understanding of the nature of the Divine. This was the first time God showed a need, a longing for love from human beings. That zeal for humanity was clear in the incarnation and again in the revelations of the Sacred Heart. They indicate that divinity *includes* longing, as was evident at the Last Supper: "I have eagerly desired to eat this Passover with you before I suffer" (Luke 22:15). This longing of God for man is a metaphor for how the Divine needs the human to incarnate its light into the world.

In Revelation, there is an image of Christ knocking at our door rather than waiting for us to seek him: "Listen! I am standing at the door, knocking; if you hear my voice and open the door, I will come in to you and eat with you, and you with me" (3:20). When this touching scene is pictured, the door is depicted with the doorknob on the inside. Our calling by Christ is thus an invitation, not a command. It is up to us to let the Divine into our lives. We see this same theme in two other biblical quotations:

> I slept, but my heart was awake. Listen! my beloved is knocking. "Open to me, my sister, my love, my dove, my perfect one; for my head is wet with dew, my locks with the drops of the night." (Song 5:2)

> Be dressed for action and have your lamps lit; be like those who are waiting for their master to return from the wedding banquet, so that they may open the door for him as soon as he comes and knocks. (Luke 12:35–36)

Divine life is not free-floating or external but relies on people and all of nature to make its presence felt. The message of the heart of Jesus is a luminous awareness of the connection between the human and the Divine. The Sacred Heart is the supreme image of the cosmos on fire with life and evolutionary movement toward more consciousness and more love. We can appreciate this bigness in the devotion to the Sacred Heart of Jesus by this reworking of the traditional morning offering:

> Jesus, I say yes to everything that happens to me today as a gift from your heart and as an opportunity to give and receive love. Thank you for the graces you beam without ceasing on me and all

the world. I dedicate everything that I think, say, feel, and do to your heart's desire: a world of justice, peace, and love.

Jesus, I now think of myself as living solely for your Sacred Heart. —Pope St. John XXIII

MARY

The Madonna and Child are God's supreme truth.
—Michelangelo

In ancient times, the Great Mother was a central deity. The worship of the Great Mother was tied to nature worship; places in nature were sacred to her: springs, grottoes, hillsides, moon, stars. The cult of Mary arose in that context though not simply in imitation of it.

Mary, in Christian times, supplanted Isis and Demeter as the archetypal figure of the Great Mother. All the pagan elements of goddesses were transferred to a new object. This is not idolatry since the psyche always knew that nature is feminine and is deserving of our honor. Nature is trusted as a mother who renews our life with the passing seasons, especially spring. May was chosen as Mary's month because it is a time of renewal, a recognition that the return of new life is reliable. We are part of nature and live in those same cycles.

In the Middle Ages, God was understood in theology as pure giving/creating and did not include a receptive side. There was also an accent on justice as requiring retribution. The psyche cannot be fooled; it always knew these were male-constructed, limited ego perspectives. The image of

Mary worked to provide what was missing in the full archetype of divinity. She receives from God and gives to us.

St. Anselm wrote, "God is the father of all created things and Mary is mother of all recreated things."[12] Devotion to the Mother of God became devotion to God as motherly. These were not theological distortions as much as archetypal recognitions. The male image of God is not sufficient and cannot satisfy the manifold longings of the human psyche. Some compensation is necessary in a masculine-ideal religion like Catholicism. It comes in the form of Mary as Mother of the Church.

To ascribe female attributes to a male God misses the point. One figure cannot accommodate all that. The feminine, the mother, is a necessary character in the full cast of divinity. The primordial knowledge of polytheism was taken literally and was unsophisticated, but the concept behind it is a solid one: divinity is a spectrum containing all the archetypal possibilities—mother, father, divine child, hero, shadow, trickster, wise guide, compassionate companion, shadow, and so forth. It is not that there are many gods but that our human/divine nature and goal is polyvalent, that is, many powered. The task of faith is not to reassign the qualities of the archetype of Mary to God but to preserve her unique place in our faith experience. Feminine energy is not a supplement to masculine energy. It is its necessary complement.

Mary is not a symbol of God's feminine side or even a personification of it; she is another figure in the pantheon required for beings as diverse and complex as ourselves. Neither male nor female divinities alone have satisfied the human soul; both are necessary. It is not that a male God is just and Mary is forgiving and holding back his just wrath. The creative and the destructive and every set of opposites coexist in the full panoply of divinity. ("Destructive" means ego-dissolving.) All are necessary and work in a harmonious axis. There is justice and mercy and advocacy in the divine masculine as well as in the divine feminine.

Today there is less accent on Mary in the Church, and this represents both a gain and a loss. It is a gain when liturgy takes precedence over devotion. However, Mary brings a necessary element to the life of faith: she represents the alchemical vessel that gestates and brings forth the Source and Redeemer of life.

Carl Jung referred to the Annunciation, the visit of the angel Gabriel to Mary, as a perfect metaphor for how the archetypal world breaks in upon our transitory universe. The angelic and the human, the male and the female, the infinite and the finite, all apparent opposites meet in that moment. This is another powerful metaphor for our own destiny to gain entry through time to the world beyond time. We acknowledge the presence of the transcendent in our little room, and we become filled with it so that we can deliver it to the world we love as Mary did before and still does.

Unfortunately, Mary is an injured archetype. What has been handed down to us in the images of Jesus and Mary lack wholeness. It is up to us to expand their images with the full powers they deserve. Mary needs to be filled out with other qualities of the female, not only motherliness and receptivity, but passion, affiliativeness, the power to renew, and intimacy. She is an inadequate archetype when she is all giving and all nurturing with no darker side. A childish need to have a mother who is only kind and never limit-setting is reflected in the traditional archetype of Mary. It is a challenge to adult faith to find the dissolving power of the Mother, to ask her to dismantle our ego.

In all cultures and times, the female was the archetype of the dissolution of the male ego. The patriarchal Church certainly needs the full experience of Mary. The archetype of the Mother of God is thus also a vehicle to describe how the Divine becomes conscious, that is, by female energy, by nurturant love, by motherly care. Mary is the archetype of the psyche itself, for it truly gives birth to God. In this sense, Mary is ourselves when the incarnation/individuation process has happened to us. She is the model of our destiny to bring to birth the Divine in the human.

Mary's human life is the fullness of grace. The dogmas of the immaculate conception of Mary and her assumption bodily into heaven do not simply delineate privileges. They tell us when she was first special and whether it ever changed. She is the exemplar of all us humans: we are radically acceptable, graced from the beginning by the graciousness of divine love. Paul Tillich spoke of God as the ground of being but he defines it as "the mother quality of giving birth, carrying, and embracing, and, at the same time, of calling back, resisting independence of the created, and swallowing it."[13] He sees both sides of the eternal Self in God. Both sides of the eternal are in Mary too.

A culture's image of Mary reflects its view of women. In the early Church, she was the model of asceticism and restraint. In medieval times, she represented courtly love, and was called the Queen of Heaven. In the nineteenth and twentieth centuries, she became the stainless ideal of harmony as a refuge from this wounded world. Yet in all times, Mary reveals the warmth in the divine life in us and toward us.

Finally, we can be touched by the simple faith of Lech Walesa, who was once recorded as saying about his Polish people, "We believe in miracles and that makes people heroes....We go to the Madonna and beg her to help us when something is very important to us." This statement reminds us that many of the rest of us may still not trust the extent of Mary's power in our world. Thomas Merton put it this way: "Where in the world has any voice / Prayed to you, Lady, for the peace that's in your power?"[14] I thought the other day how I could pray to Mary to end the conflict in the Middle East. I realized I did not imagine she could make that happen. Then I knew I did not know her yet.

O Holy, Blessed Lady,
Constant comfort to humankind.
Whose beneficience and kindness nourish us all;
And whose care for those in trouble is as a loving Mother
Who cares for all Her children - You are there when we call.
Stretching out Your hand to put aside that which is harmful to us,
Untangling the web of Fate in which we may be caught,
Even stopping the stars if they form a harmful pattern.

—*Roman Prayer to Isis by Apuleius*

THE DIVINE CHILD

In the image of the Primordial Child, the world finds its own childhood, and everything that sunrise and the birth of a child mean for and say about the world. The childhood and orphan's fate of the child gods have not evolved from the stuff of human life but from cosmic life. What appears to be biographical in mythology is an anecdote from the world biography....The child archetype represents the precious childhood aspect of the cosmic psyche. —Carl Jung

The divine child motif in the hero story provides a striking symbol of the divine/human archetype and of the archetype of transformation. He or she is the image of the Divine that has come to be an assisting and effective resource in our battle with our ego-fears and attachments. The divine child represents completed individuation, that is, our showing in the here and now the wholeness that has always been in us. That wholeness is God within, Christ consciousness, indwelling Spirit.

This archetype is not the inner child of psychology, but the inner potential of the spiritual power that wants to be born in us from the ashes of ego-centeredness. The image of the helpless infant who is nonetheless a hero shows that our limitations and terrors enclose a hidden liveliness, a bud that wants to flower. That bud blooms into cosmo-centeredness. This journey from ego-centeredness to cosmo-centeredness is the journey of faith. The divine child archetype shows us how it begins and what it forecasts.

The divine child represents the hero archetype in its infancy. He is often an orphan who is unwelcome at birth. Examples of this are Moses, Jesus, Dionysus, Horus. All these heroes were hidden after being born until it was safe for them to emerge and surprise the world with their true identity. They were cared for by women during this hidden or endangered phase of their life. This is a metaphor for the times in our life when we have to be taken care of, be hidden away, lie low until the time is right, be nurtured by the anima, the soul. It is thus a time presided over by feminine graceful energies of grace rather than ego-effort.

Mary is the personification of those energies. We find Mary's warmest meaning when we let ourselves feel held in the dark by a maternal force of tenderness. That is a powerful and authentically consoling way to reclaim the riches Mary was always holding out to us in our religious past. The divine child survives because of this holding from his mother.

The divine infant is isolated but ultimately he joins everyone together. In his creative dimension, the divine child is the risk taker. In his dependency, he is the needy and imperilled waif. He is vulnerable and this is how he eventually empowers himself and those he came to serve. These are the paradoxes that show us we have ventured into the spiritual world, the world where opposites unite, a helpless babe helps supremely. This is the world of Everest, at the summit of which one finds marine limestone, and where the top of the world was once the bottom of the sea.

The divine child is the cosmic wholeness that includes and expands consciousness, as a child includes his past genetic history and grows into his fuller future with time. The miraculous powers of the divine child and his resolute will to live symbolize our own psyche's vital urge toward individuation. The liveliness of a child is a perfect symbol for the yearning in us for self-realization, self-actualization, fulfillment of destiny, completion of life tasks, and contribution to the evolution of our species. The divine child thus represents the combination of all opposites. His miraculous powers and his painful bruises figure in the heroic story of humankind.

Here are the mythic characteristics of the divine child, recognizable from hero stories we know:

- His birth is miraculous, for example, virgin birth or dual birth: one parent is human; one is divine. This motif is psychic and metaphorical, not empirical or literal. It is about the ego/Self axis.

We lose the power of an archetypal event when we take it literally. It can become magic when it represents only one unique historical event in which only one person is actualized. When it is appreciated as a metaphor, it gives us oracular information about the design, potential, and destiny of everyone's psyche. Since mythology was the first psychology, the hero stories were vehicles for an understanding of who we really are and what we were meant to become. The primal archetypal event is not limited then to one moment in time or to one special hero but is happening at every moment in every one of us. There is only one story and it is ours.

- As darkness rises to protect itself, adversity befalls the divine child: "Then it goes and brings seven other spirits more evil than itself, and they enter and live there" (Luke 11:26). This is actually a good sign; evil is losing its grip and so it unleashes all its final weaponry against a force that, though fragile, has an irrepressible power. That which is about to become extinct exaggerates itself just prior to extinction. But the miraculous birth wants to happen. We have the momentum of evolution on our side. Something more than ego strives for wholeness and will not, cannot be stopped.
- The infant is at once solitary and at home in the primeval world: "He came to what was his own, and his own people did not accept him" (John 1:11). Few may welcome his birth, and yet all are in need of it. Jesus was welcomed by the Magi and the shepherds but hated by Herod. Moses was

hunted for death by the Pharaoh but welcomed by Pharaoh's sister. Horus was hidden in the papyrus swamp and cared for by Isis, who protected him from Set, the shadow god, who wanted to destroy him. Dionysus was disguised as a girl and guarded by Queen Ino when Hera sought his life.

- The ultimate triumph of the hero over the monster is a metaphor for the victory of consciousness over unconscious forces. Individuation requires a struggle. During the struggle, the hero—we Pinocchios—strike at the foe, strike out, fall into the void, are cared for by others, and are revived by a grace beyond our own making. We finally learn that the foe is within us and that friendship, not extinction, is the true goal of the work. This is why Jesus, Buddha, and the Dalai Lama are greater heroes than film idols, who can kill the foe but cannot redeem him or reconcile with him and therefore never enrich themselves with his strengths. To kill off our religious past results in the same losses.
- The divine child is often abandoned by his friends at the beginning and end of his life. Since a child is always growing toward independence, detachment along the way is necessary. Abandonment is a painful but sometimes necessary passage to this possibility. The abandoned child is the archetype of the part of us that is exposed and throws itself onto the mercy of the world. Such vulnerability is not victimization; it is ultimately empowering. The willingness to take one's chances confers the power. This rugged courage,

like superior awareness, will feel like orphan aloneness throughout life. Yet higher consciousness is only possible in the context of such isolation and vulnerability.

- The paradox of the divine child is in his holding of two major opposites that plague us in life: vulnerability and power. To be stuck in fear is to be victimized by fear. We then do not hold both sides. Achilles is a personification of the courageous human ability to hold vulnerability and power simultaneously. His story acknowledges the wonderfully accommodating nature of the psyche and violates none of its multiple qualities. Uniting opposites is the emblem of the child-hero as well as the central thrust of the work of befriending the dark side. Dorothy united the images of the simple farm hands and the heroic-assisting forces of her journey through Oz. She thus endowed their lowliness with glory, adorning and transforming their weakness into strength. Dorothy's vulnerability led to a daring spontaneity, just what it took to dissolve the witch's power and then to share it with her friends. She represents the divine child's power to participate in the flow of life consciously, no matter how beset with griefs, with no need to destroy it. *Can we embark on such a perilous voyage?*

Our gracious Creator cares and provides for all His creatures. His tender mercies are over all His works, and so far as His love influences our minds, so far as we become interested in His workmanship, and feel a desire to take hold of every opportunity to lessen the distresses of the afflicted and to increase the happiness of the creation.
Here we have a prospect of one common interest from which our own is inseparable, so that to turn all that we possess into the channel of universal love becomes the business of our lives.

—John Woolman: *The Quaker Journal*

CHAPTER FIVE

Taking a Stand with Jesus

Bless those who persecute you; bless and do not curse them. Rejoice with those who rejoice, weep with those who weep. Live in harmony with one another; do not be haughty, but associate with the lowly; do not claim to be wiser than you are. Do not repay anyone evil for evil, but take thought for what is noble in the sight of all. If it is possible, so far as it depends on you, live peaceably with all. Beloved, never avenge yourselves....Do not be overcome by evil, but overcome evil with good.

—Romans 12:14–19, 21

In this passage, Jesus' teaching matches and awakens the deepest and most enduring of human possibilities: to love without reserve. Jesus shows us a new way of living beyond what ego comes up with, a new way of designing our behavior beyond the style of a violent world. When the law of

Christ lives in us, our ego enters the service of a higher life. We join him in subverting the old paradigm of revenge by our commitment to reconciliation, of hate by our choice to love, and of death by our dedication to life.

THE SERMON ON THE MOUNT

Love your enemies,
do good to those who hate you,
bless those who curse you,
pray for those who abuse you. —Luke 6:27–28

The Sermon on the Mount is the new paradigm of human relating. It describes unconditional love in practical terms. It spells out exactly how the grandiose, narcissistic ego can be transcended. Real faith always leads to love and love is only possible when our ego-centeredness takes a bow. In the Sermon on the Mount, Jesus spares no hideout or disguise of ego in his razor-sharp delineation of what love means. He reverses the definitions of honor and shame.

Honor (saving face) and shame (losing face) were the two central concerns in the ancient world. In the Sermon on the Mount (Matthew 5—7) and Sermon on the Plain (Luke 6), Jesus reverses them: what was shameful is honorable and what was honorable is shameful. We see this especially in the Beatitudes. The world of those who are in positions of power and influence say that the destitute are to be looked down on. Jesus says the oppressed are blessed, the lowly will be rewarded, and the persecuted will inherit.

Here is an example of the pre–Christian view. Aristotle wrote in his *Rhetoric*, "To take just revenge on enemies and refuse to be reconciled is praiseworthy; for to retaliate is just." Jesus recommends the opposite: "So when you are offering your gift at the altar, if you remember that your brother or sister has something against you, leave your gift there before the altar and go; first be reconciled to your brother or sister, and then come and offer your gift" (Matt 5:23–24). That plan would be considered cowardly and shameful in the ancient view. Revenge is the appropriate reaction to any insult, otherwise one is looked down on as being weak. That is the public's verdict on anyone who chooses reconciliation rather than retribution.

Jesus, however, condemns retaliation in any form. Thus, the sermon proposes not only changing one's behavior but opening oneself to shame in society, where not retaliating is a sign of weakness. It is doubly painful to follow this teaching: We have to make allowances and forgive when our primitive reflex is to retaliate. We have to open ourselves to being looked down on by others, to be seen as foolish and weak.

If a person insulted another in the world of power and privilege, it gave him the right to avenge his honor. Jesus puts a stop to the habitual honor game and blood feuding. He speaks against vindicating oneself at another's expense. Instead he tells his followers to go and reconcile, to change hostility to friendliness.

The content of the Sermon on the Mount is derived from the Hebrew Scriptures and rabbinical teaching. However, we do see a difference between some views expressed in the Hebrew Scriptures and the Beatitudes within the sermon. For instance, many psalms complain to God for letting the chosen people lose face or be the laughingstock of the pagans. The psalmist complains about what Christ recommends! Compare, for example, Psalm 44:13–16:

You have made us the taunt of our neighbors,
the derision and scorn of those around us.
You have made us a byword among the nations,
a laughingstock among the peoples.
All day long my disgrace is before me,
and shame has covered my face
at the words of the taunters and revilers,
at the sight of the enemy and the avenger.

The psalmist asks God to uphold his ego, "Do not let me lose face." The Sermon on the Mount asks God to help us let go of ego, to welcome losing face for the sake of our commitment to Christ. We see this alternative described in Matthew:

> "Blessed are those who are persecuted for righteousness' sake, for theirs is the kingdom of heaven. Blessed are you when people revile you and persecute you and utter all kinds of evil against you falsely on my account. Rejoice and be glad, for your reward is great in heaven, for in the same way they persecuted the prophets who were before you." (5:10–12)

We see the same Christ alternative to the indignant ego also in the writings of Paul:

> For I think that God has exhibited us apostles as last of all, as though sentenced to death, because we have become a spectacle to the world, to angels and to mortals. We are fools for the sake of Christ, but you are wise in Christ. We are weak, but you are strong. You are held in honor, but we in disrepute. To the present hour we are hungry

> and thirsty, we are poorly clothed and beaten and homeless, and we grow weary from the work of our own hands. When reviled, we bless; when persecuted, we endure; when slandered, we speak kindly. We have become like the rubbish of the world, the dregs of all things, to this very day. (1 Cor 4:9–13)

The new covenant includes a calling to live the life story of Jesus in our lifetime. This is not the ego's story of protection from losing face, but the dedicated-to-love journey to a new kind of life. John Dominic Crossan states that Jesus had a "strategy for building or rebuilding…community on radically different principles from those of honor and shame."[1] The Word became flesh; that is to say the divine meaning of life, is incarnated in a certain human way of living. That way of living can be summarized in the basic recommendations of the Sermon on the Mount:

- Seeking reconciliation and forgiveness
- Choosing nonviolence in disputes
- Living by example not coercion
- Being generous
- Returning good for evil, blessing for curse, love for hate, and compassion for hurt
- Respecting love and wisdom over position and wealth
- Letting go of anxiety about how things will turn out
- Letting go of judgment and competitiveness

These principles represent wholeness in human living because they are ways of loving that encompass the full spectrum of our human capability. They are steps in the dismantling of an arrogant ego and the granting of strength and choice to an impoverished, victimized ego. Morality for an adult means exactly this kind of reversal. We are then no longer under the influence of fear or neediness, for we have found the path that transforms the self-defeating and love-defeating habits of ego.

Psychological adulthood means building a healthy ego, one that is functional, that is, works to bring us to our goal of effective and happy living and relating. At the same time, our psychological work is to let go of the neurotic ego with its insistence on control and entitlement, qualities that shut the door on effective and happy living and relating. The Sermon on the Mount is the recipe for letting go of ego.

It seems that all of us can practice the directives in the Sermon on the Mount, but it takes a special grace and a deep surrender to live it out fully and courageously, and to put ourselves on the line for it. This is why it is a spiritual calling, not only a personal psychological enterprise. It is also to be applied to our collective lives as members of any human community, whether family or work related.

Courage, or any virtue, is a gift of grace. When we find ourselves doing something courageous, we can therefore show gratitude as our spiritual practice. This recognition of a link between virtue and grace helps us appreciate our value in the world. We realize that our growth in virtue is important to a higher power that is helping us evolve. We behold the evolution in the result of our brave action: our soul has widened so we no longer fit into the old fear-based mold of who we were. In addition, our gratitude is not only thanks; it is a contact and communion with the source of grace. Such nearness to the Divine is how we evolve spiritually.

The following is a practice of affirmations that opens us to the moral transformations implicit in the Sermon on the Mount. As with all affirmations, they support rather than replace active, visible, behavioral change. *It may be helpful to notice which ones resonate for you. Write out and say (as often as you choose throughout the day) the ones that strike you.*

I am the rightful heir to all the earth has to give.
I accept the conditions of existence as opportunities to show more love.
I release more and more compassion into my world.
The universe is benevolent to me.
I am pure of heart and see God.
I make peace and am a child of God.
I acknowledge pain and persecution as part of life.
I let go of the need to punish or to take revenge.
I let go of fearing God as punitive but trust in inexhaustible divine mercy.
I let go of the need to get back at anyone.
I let go of the need to get even with anyone.
I let go of the need to correct others' impressions of me.
I choose reconciliation.
I let go of my grudges.
I let go of the need to be right or to be justified.
I admit when I am wrong and apologize.
I let go of stubbornness and rigidity.
I let go of the need to control others.
I am comfortable with the power in humility.
I let go of perfectionism; I am perfect as I am.
I drop the need to be the center of attention.

I am open to criticism and feedback.
I look for what is true and build on it.
I look for the good and praise it.
I appreciate myself and take care of myself.
I release myself from shame, guilt, and self-blame.
I choose gentleness in all my affairs.
I let go of my belief in the effectiveness in violence.
I let go of the use of or collaboration with violence.
I drop the use of put-downs, insults, or sarcasm.
I love those who hate me.
I bless those who curse me.
I do good to those who hurt me.
I help others care for themselves.
I let go of anxiety about survival and security.
I let go of judging others.
If others judge me or make fun of me for following Christ's teaching, I realize I am on the spiritual path and I pray for their conversion.
I am always on the way to the light.
I let the light through.
I release love, wisdom, and healing into the universe and receive it too.

THE RADIANT VIRTUES OF JESUS

The Sermon on the Mount shows us what Christ is like. We are asked to be God-centered as he was. So he is not only a great teacher and exemplar. He also gives us the grace to follow his teaching, even to suffering and death. In that sense, more is going on in being a Christian than simply following a teacher. A teacher teaches. Christ gives us the gift of following his teaching at any cost. A teacher shows the way. Christ is the way. A teacher shows the value of a certain behavior. Christ gives us the power to put it into practice.

The following are some virtues that Jesus lived by. To be devoted to Jesus is to live in this same way. Everyone receives the grace to do so. We now see that devotion is to the lifestyle of Jesus, not to an icon of him.

To trust in God as a parent/companion who is not distant but a presence within us.

To vow ourselves to nonviolence and non-retaliation, putting our accent on restorative, not retributive, justice.

Never to give up on others as God does not give up on us: even at the eleventh hour any prodigal son can be reconciled. The prodigal son was welcomed home before he showed any sign of contrition. There was no condition that had to be fulfilled as a prerequisite to restoring the connection between him and his father.

To perform the works of mercy: feed the hungry, clothe the naked, find homes for the homeless, and visit the sick and imprisoned.

To reverse worldly values so that ego status, financial gain, political prestige, and control are not as important as love. Jesus put no accent on money, property, or power, often the conspicuous concerns of institutions, including churches. He distrusted these as distractions from the new values he lived by: generosity, simplicity, and compassion.

To abolish divisions, ranks, or distinctions that separate, to have no biases against those who are different because of gender, race, color, belief, or sexual orientation. If we retain prejudices against those who are different from us, then Christian faith has not yet taken effect in us, nor has the Eucharist.

To speak truth to power and to confront hypocrisy fearlessly but compassionately, including our own.

To make an unconditional commitment to a life of love and forgiveness no matter how we are treated by others.

To trust that the grace to do all this is always available and abundant.

A CONSCIENCE THAT TAKES ACTION

Grave inequalities within and among nations are automatically suspect in Catholic thinking and constitute not the legitimate natural order but a profound violation of that order.

—Bishop Robert W. McElroy, "Market Assumptions," in *America*, November 3, 2014

There is a Sufi saying: "Generosity means doing justice without first requiring justice."[2] Every religious tradition has a teacher with the same recommendations as in Christ's Sermon on the Mount. Through the ages, there has been a living tradition of nonviolence and of generous love. Every religion has produced saints who kept this tradition alive—a striking way of describing tradition. Here is an example of a commitment to nonviolence from Jesuit John Dear, in his statement in court in 2007:

> It's a powerful experience to stand before a judge and be sentenced to jail for saying No to war, injustice and nuclear weapons, something I highly recommend for all followers of the nonviolent Jesus.

> It really helps clarify one's discipleship, one's citizenship in God's reign of peace, one's faith, hope and love. In these days of war, genocide, nuclear weapons, poverty, executions, abortion, torture, global warming, and violence of every description, it's a great grace to be in trouble with the empire for practicing nonviolence, for daring to offer a word of peace, for serving the God of peace.[3]

Some of us were taught to believe in a God made in the image of human ego, one with an unalterable insistence on punishment and reward. The ego gods are primitive and ungenerous. The identity Jesus reveals is based on love, not fear. A life-enhancing, updated faith is one that shows, exemplifies, and teaches the egoless and fearless love that Jesus lived. This is how we share in Christ's divinity. The statement of Jesus that says, "Take courage; I have conquered the world!" (John 16:33), means the heart of Christ has overcome the ego in us. Ego is the source of fear, so letting go of it is freedom from fear. The higher Self has overcome.

This letting go means that our ego bows to our higher Self, which makes challenging demands. We would have to be willing to surrender what has buoyed us up for so much of our life. We would have to move from street style to Jesus style. Our dedication to Christ's law won't be pretty in the eyes of others who will see us as foolish. It won't be safe because others might take advantage of our humility or harm us for it. This is why the call of Christ in the Sermon on the Mount is so unappealing to most of us. Yet the only response from Christ is "Take courage; I have conquered the world!" In other words, "I can convert to my heart the street, the bullies, the nations." All we have is that promise; we are called to trust in it.

Our spirituality is progressing when our *first reaction* to others is not from our ego-mind, but from the heart of Christ, our true nature, who we really are. Thus the ego's automatic reaction of conditioned love can become unconditional love; narrow ego biases can become expansive and generous wisdom; retaliation can vanish into reconciliation. Our first impulse is not to get back *at* but to get back *with*. Through practice, that new set of Christ-responses becomes habitual. That habit is called sanctity, the holiness of wholeness. Our larger, higher, deeper identity has triumphed over the limiting but sheltering habits of ego.

As our life becomes more aligned to the Sermon on the Mount, our devotedness to Christ acts itself out in ways that show abiding commitment to world concerns. We are committed to fighting injustice in nonviolent ways. True faith leads to progressively higher consciousness of the link between religion and responsiveness to the needs of all people. It does not begin or end in church. It begins in the heart and ends in the real world. It is a letting go of the primacy of ego gratification in favor of the investment and subjection of our ego for the good of all.

If I say I believe in the resurrection, for example, but do not shape my life in accord with that belief—translate it into personal and other-directed action—it exists solely in my mind. I am giving what Cardinal Newman called "notional assent" instead of "real assent."[4] Authentic faith means real assent, that is, what is internally held is externally manifested. For example, to shape my life in accord with belief in the resurrection means, first of all, that I am personally free from fear. St. Peter, before the resurrection, feared a powerless serving-girl. After it, he defied authorities that had the power to kill him.

Here are statements of a committed faith in the resurrection that demonstrate how it can have effects in daily life and manifest our wholeness—the culmination of living the life of Christ in the world. To say that Jesus is alive is to affirm:

I have nothing left to fear and I act that way even when I feel fear.
I am detached from worldly gain and act that way.
I am free from fearful obsessions about death and act that way.
My life has a worth that does not have to be earned.
My awareness of all this makes me joyous in good times and helps me handle tough times effectively and optimistically.
I share this news not by persuading or proving but by word and deed.
I have changed and keep changing.

These statements provide examples of how an internal belief can be integrated into our daily life experience. To have faith in a big-hearted way is to create a congruence between every belief and behavior. This means there is no longer a dichotomy between personal psychological work and spiritual practice. There is no longer a dichotomy between ourselves and nature. There is no longer a difference between loving ourselves and loving others. It is all one experience of individuation that honors our human-divine nature. Big-hearted faith is a faith of equations not divisions.

We recall Isaiah 58:6:

Is not this the fast that I choose:
to loose the bonds of injustice,
to undo the thongs of the yoke,
to let the oppressed go free,
and to break every yoke?

As we embrace the bigness of our faith commitment—its cosmic dimensions—we put less accent on individualistic salvation ("Jesus and I") and more accent on redeeming the planet. Jesus told us what collective salvation consisted of:

The Spirit of the Lord is upon me,
because he has anointed me to bring good news to the poor.
He has sent me to proclaim release to the captives
and recovery of sight to the blind, to let the oppressed go free,
to proclaim the year of the Lord's favor.
(Luke 4:18–19)

This is all about the needs of a here and now world. The statement is a release from fatalism, the belief that things can't get better, that oppression and injustice can't be reduced. A prophetic imagination, our universal calling, defies that limited view. Thus, the redemption of the world is release from injustice in our time in every nation and political arena. Pope Benedict XVI wrote, "What has Jesus really brought…if he has not brought world peace, universal prosperity, and a better world?"

Joseph Martos shows the connection between this sense of the bigness of salvation and the sacraments:

> As long as the Gospel and the sacraments are not seen as referring to salvation in this life and the transformation of the world into God's kingdom, the oppressed peoples of the earth will never fully realize the freedom of God's sons and daughters for which Jesus died and for which the Church was founded. For sacraments concretely symbolize what they abstractly stand for only when in the course of their performance they make what they represent experientially and personally present in sacred space and time.[5]

The more we see ourselves as part of a Mystical Body—the human community—the more we care about its fate and history. Faith becomes truly mature in the same way that relationships become mature: we see beyond our own narcissistic needs and offer someone beyond ourselves our love and attention. Social, political, and ecological consciousness joined with action is the style of cosmic consciousness. In it we have transcended narrow personal limits and love limitlessly. There is a quotation of Ghandi that states, "I do not believe that the spiritual law works on a field of its own. On the contrary it expresses itself only through the ordinary activities of life. It thus affects the economic, the social and the political fields."[6] Values for a person of faith are consistently applied to social concerns. This is taking a stand with Jesus.

Our life of faith as a heroic journey is both communal and personal. We tread the path already trod by our ancestors in faith and we blaze our own path. We are followers *and* pioneers. The greatest challenge of big-hearted faith is to venture outside the ordinary, outside the tried and true, to our own unique configuration of the mystery into which we will be initiated. The second greatest challenge is to honor our faith inheritance at the same time. This book has focused on how to do both.

A big-hearted faith has made a radical difference in our way of seeing the world, our way of being in it, and our way of caring for it. Cosmic faith makes a radical difference in how we live, how we love, how we think. It is entirely rooted in the principles of the Sermon on the Mount. Only when love makes all the difference does religion have meaning. St. Aelred, a twelfth-century English abbot, states,

> You are good and lovable as you are. God is Friendship and all the loves of your life are part of that great friendship for which you are eternally destined....Create a small piece of paradise here on earth by loving and embracing each other and by loving and embracing the whole world. The cruelty, chaos, and pain of daily living cannot dim your vision of everlasting, perfect love as long as you stay true to your precious friendships.[7]

The spiritual journey is not from point A (our sinfulness) to point B (our redemption). It is all one emancipative journey of continually mended failures, reunion, and transformation. Our journey is from here to Here, from the here and now of our lives to the wider Here and Now of our destiny. This is how we create conditions "on earth as it is in Heaven."

Once there is room for all humankind in the heart of each of us, our work will not be to convince others of "the truth" but to bring the Church, that is, our best selves, to the world and to include the world in its embrace. Our struggle will not be to evangelize in the sense of proselytizing but to evangelize in the sense of bringing love everywhere. Such good news is really an awareness of precisely what makes the message of Jesus so radical and encouraging: salvation of ourselves happens through love of others. This is being saved from fear and finding love amid any ruins.

Finally, taking a stand with Jesus is a call to show the limitless dimensions of our social concerns. The following passages taken from an encyclical by Pope Paul VI, *Populorum Progressio*, "On the Development of Peoples," written in 1967, encourage and show us how to expand our faith to cosmic size:

> The hungry nations of the world cry out to the peoples blessed with abundance. And the Church, cut to the quick by this cry, asks each and every person to hear his brother's plea and answer it lovingly.

> Now if the earth truly was created to provide people with the necessities of life and the tools for his own progress, it follows that every person has the right to glean what he needs from the earth....Thus, under the leadership of justice and

in the company of charity, created goods should flow fairly to all.

No one may appropriate surplus goods solely for his own private use when others lack the bare necessities of life.

It is not just a question of eliminating hunger and reducing poverty. It involves building a human community where liberty is not an idle word, where the needy Lazarus can sit down with the rich man at the same banquet table.

Each person must examine his conscience, which sounds a new call in our present times. Is he prepared to support, at his own expense, projects and undertakings designed to help the needy? Is he prepared to pay higher taxes so that public authorities may expand their efforts in the work of development? Is he prepared to pay more for imported goods, so that the foreign producer may make a fairer profit? Is he prepared to emigrate from his homeland if necessary and if he is young, in order to help the emerging nations?

No one is permitted to disregard the plight of his brothers living in dire poverty, enmeshed in ignorance and tormented by insecurity. The Christian, moved by this sad state of affairs, should echo the words of Christ: "I have compassion on the multitude."

If science and technology are ever to be liberated from tutelage to the dominative powers of history, if the drama is to be "interrupted" redemptively rather than destructively, then Christian theology, which has itself been enticed time and again to legitimate dominative power, can contribute to that future by mediating more dialectically to the present the subversive memories of God's identification with the struggles of victims everywhere in the mystery and message of Christ Jesus.

—Matthew Lamb, "Liberation Theology and Social Justice," *Process Studies* 14, no. 2 (Summer 1985): 102–22

Epilogue

Our Spiritual Heritage

We are in grave danger of losing a spiritual heritage that has been painfully accumulated by thousands of generations of saints and contemplatives....To cling to one partial view....and to treat this as the ultimate answer to all questions is simply to... make oneself obdurate in error.

—Thomas Merton,
The Asian Journal of Thomas Merton

We can leave a church or abandon religious practices, but we cannot leave our psyche, which goes on proclaiming the same revelations that religions do. Something, we know not what or how, is always at work bringing the good news to life. Religions are mediums of an abiding and irrepressible truth in the interior life of humankind.

Our psyche is not limited to our cranium. Intrapsychic means omnipsychic, cosmopsychic. Psyche in that context is understood as inclusive of every human being and of the universe: "Heaven *and earth* are full of your glory." Soul is thus not limited to humans. The world soul is a metaphor for how all of nature has a divine destiny and meaning. Meaning does not have to be configured as simply a device of the human mind. All the world is finding, showing, and making meanings too.

It is now perhaps clear that we have an interactive psyche; a personal aliveness within a world aliveness. It takes both to construct a richly complete human experience. There can be no inner life separate from the natural world. Likewise the world is continually influenced by our inner life. In the communion of saints, all of us are at the effect of each of us. This applies to us in the natural world too. As we have seen in the previous chapters, we have a larger life than ego or our past or even the past of our species. Our being is not an individual unit but part of an ecology, a cosmic reality. We are always both autonomous and related.

Evolution has been leading to more and more synthesis. It is the ongoing synthesis of the world and ourselves, no longer in opposition but in collaboration. All that is required on our part is that we no longer operate from an "I/It" position to the world but an "I/Thou" relationship. Like God, the cosmos is not wholly other but who we are inherently. It is not that all are the same but all are one: my spirit, the world spirit, the Holy Spirit. To deny our unity and communion is thus to diminish the dimensions of ourselves and our world.

The forces of nature faithfully and continually cooperate. The rainforests of Hawaii, for instance, are nurtured by minerals from the sands of the Gobi desert of China, blown there by the winds. An advantage of life in the mystical Christ is finding the numinosity of the universe. Romantic poets were among the first to see the transcendental consciousness of nature, continually creative and animating all of us. Mystics like Hildegaard of Bingen saw it centuries earlier. Similarly, the mystic, Nicholas of Cusa, in *On the Pursuit of Wisdom*, wrote, "The divine is the enfolding of the universe, and the universe is the unfolding of the divine."

The world is not only being created but creating. The universe is creative in that it is continually engaged in producing more highly organized wholes. This zeal for unity without canceling diversity is what is meant by evolution, the way creation happens. "Let there be light," did not simply happen but, like all revelations, is a happening that is happening now. "Now" happens whenever ego gets out of the way long enough to let the light through.

Karl Rahner speaks of "the silent mystery that tastes like nothingness because it is infinity."[1] This foundation of spaciousness in the psyche exactly mirrors the ground of the galaxies and pure space. Any conscious spiritual view is a metaphor for a physical reality. Every key belief in religion has a natural analogue. For instance, resurrection has resonance in the rebirth of the earth in spring. Nature houses religious truths through the centuries, like cathedrals that are houses of God but can only be built of natural wood and stone.

The Council of Chalcedon proclaimed the two natures of Christ, human and divine, in one person. This is a declaration about us too. Our psychic maturation involves gradual realization of an unceasing continuity between human and divine. This is expressed well by Raimondo Panikkar: "The Christian vision today has lost its foundation inasmuch as it lacks an adequate cosmovision....God is the transcendent mystery immanent in us....Is not divinity infinite life in eternal participation more than a supreme individual Being?…'In him the fullness of divinity dwells bodily' (Col 2:9). This is the human vocation."[2] This is how Chalcedon can forecast the intuitions of who we are now that we have found our true cosmology.

Finally, the human-divine vocation is visible as a metaphor in a perennial religious practice—pilgrimage. We were born as pilgrims, not tourists. We know our life is a pilgrimage, a journey, because we can see farther than we can reach. Whether to Delphi or Lourdes, human beings travel to shrines for healing of body and renewal of spirit. A shrine seems to represent an external God. Actually, it is a crossroads of divinity and humanity. It focuses our attention on a power that abides both beyond us and in us. A shrine is a window. We look at the image enshrined and we glimpse the Divine. Yet a shrine is also a mirror. In it we see a reflection of our own calling, the divine potential for wholeness in every one of us. Graces come to match and expand our unknown and unacknowledged capacities: "Your faith has made you whole." The shrine shows the path *and* the paradise promising a future that has already happened and that wants to happen again—when Catholic means cosmic.

The All is wholly within us and even then seems wholly without us….It is an object infinitely great and ravishing: as full of treasures as full of room, as full of joy as of capacity.

—Thomas Traherne, a seventeenth century Anglican mystic, *Centuries of Meditation*

APPENDIX

Eucharistic Prayer of the Cosmic Christ

We thank you, God of fatherly and motherly love:
We thank you for sending us word about yourself in nature, in humanity, in words,
and finally in the eternal Word, Jesus Christ,
the universal human conceived by the Holy Spirit
and born in flesh from one of us, Mary,
now our heavenly Mother and Queen of the Universe.
We thank you for Jesus Christ, present among and in us now.
He gathers us together in this sacrament he designed
to show us how to love not only our near and dear
but all humans everywhere, without exception or bias,
and to show a caring connection to all the natural world.

With hands extended

Fatherly and motherly God, send your Holy Spirit to consecrate these gifts of bread and wine, that they may become for us the body † and the blood † of our Lord Jesus Christ, the spiritual food that makes us one mystical body with one sacred heart.

On the eve of his passion and death, showing us the uttermost proof of his love and desiring so fervently to be with us always, Jesus was at table with those he cared so much for—this table where he joins us still.

On that night, he took bread and gave you thanks †
he broke the bread, gave it to his disciples, and said:

TAKE THIS, ALL OF YOU, AND EAT IT.
THIS IS MY BODY GIVEN FOR YOU.

When supper was ended, he took the cup;
again, he gave you thanks †
and, handing the cup to his disciples, he said:

TAKE THIS, ALL OF YOU, AND DRINK FROM IT.
THIS IS THE CUP OF MY BLOOD,
THE BLOOD OF THE NEW AND EVERLASTING COVENANT.
IT WILL BE SHED FOR YOU AND FOR ALL
TO HEAL ALL DIVISIONS AND TO SHOW MY LIMITLESS LOVE.
DO THIS IN MEMORY OF ME.

Let us proclaim the mystery of faith:
Christ has died, Christ is risen, Christ will come again.

And so, God of all holiness, we celebrate the memory and mystery of Christ, our Brother, whom you led through suffering and death to the glory of resurrection and ascension, still happening now and every day, in all of us, by the grace of your Holy Spirit.

You see how our hearts are burning within us now because we are celebrating, with all-exceeding joy, the Passover mystery that Jesus accomplished and entrusted to us.

We pray for our pope, bishops, priests, and deacons.

Let your ministers, male and female, and all your Church, stand out, as courageous witnesses to freedom, justice, equality, and peace.

May we be a comfort to this troubled world, a light where there is darkness, a force of hope where there is despair, a source of love where there is hate and ignorance.

We invoke those saintly and brave humans whom we admire and commit ourselves to imitating.

May they guide us as fellow members of the communion of saints.

Please mention those you admire as saints, living or dead.

Lord, be mindful of our brothers and sisters who have died and whose faith only you can know.

Please mention the names of those who have died so they can participate with us in this Eucharist.

Lead them to the fullness of the resurrection and gladden them with the light of your presence.

May your mercy gather and save all humanity in the consummation of history, when your Son will come in the glory of the Holy Spirit with a heart open wide enough to include us all.

All-loving God, when our own pilgrimage on earth is complete, welcome us into your heavenly home.

There, with Mary, the Mother of God and of all of us, with St. Joseph, our protector, with the apostles, the martyrs, and all the saints, we shall praise you and spend our heaven doing good for those still here on earth.

Ever-creating, ever-renewing God, we thank you for this moment of Pentecost when your Holy Spirit comes upon us so we can live the life of Jesus on earth, with tender care for all humanity and with enthusiasm for the evolution of our planet.

This is our exultant calling, our life purpose, our sacred trust, our evolutionary destiny, and our richest grace.

Now we have the name and hold the heart of Jesus so

Through him, †
with him, †
and in him, †
in the unity of the Holy Spirit, all glory and honor is yours, almighty Father,
for ever and ever.

ALL: *Amen.*

PRAYER AFTER COMMUNION

Thank you God for showing us in this Eucharist who we really are: a unity of body and spirit, human and divine, without division, without exclusion of anyone or anything, for all is sacred.

When you look at us, you see us in the loving heart of your Son who makes us all one, not only those of us here at this table but all humanity around the table of the universe.

We have partaken of the body of the risen Christ, because we are his Body and so is this whole world.

Now send us forth to continue your work of evolving the Church and the world.

We thank you for creating the universe and each of us, through Christ the pioneer of our journey, and in the Holy Spirit, the gift of your love, one God forever and ever.

ALL: *Amen.*

Notes

INTRODUCTION

1. St. Cyril of Jerusalem, "Catechetical Lectures of St. Cyril of Jerusalem," XIII, no. 28.

2. Athanasius, *De incarnatione Verbi Dei* 54, 3: PG 25, 192B.

3. Thomas Keating, *Open Mind, Open Heart: The Contemplative Dimension of the Gospel* (New York: Continuum, 1994), 127.

4. Yanns Tzifopoulos, *Paradise Earned: The Bacchic-Orphic Gold Lamellae of Crete* (Cambridge, MA: Harvard University Center for Hellenic Studies, 2010), chap. 3.

CHAPTER ONE

1. Judy Cannato, *Field of Compassion: How the New Cosmology Is Transforming Spiritual Life* (South Bend, IN: Sorin Books, 2010), 59–60.

2. Alan Watts, *The Book: On the Taboo of Knowing Who You Are* (New York: Vintage Books, 1989).

3. Paul Tillich, *Systematic Theology* (Chicago: University of Chicago Press), 1:245.

4. Our references to the higher Self in this book are meant in this sense.

5. Origen, *Homilies on Leviticus, 1–16* (Washington, DC: CUA Press, 2010), 92.

6. Peter L. Berger, *A Rumor of Angels: Modern Society and the Rediscovery of the Supernatural* (New York: Doubleday, 1970), 52ff.

7. Cited by Avery Dulles in "The Ignatian Experience in the Theology of Karl Rahner." Originally from "Ueber die Erfahrung der Gnade," *Schriften* III, 108.

8. See also *Catachism of the Catholic Church,* I, 293: St. Bonaventure explains that God created all things "not to increase his glory, but to show it forth and to communicate it." St. Bonaventure, *In II Sent.* I, 2, 2, 1.

9. Bruno Borchert, *Mysticism: Its History and Challenge* (York Beach, ME: Samuel Weiser, 1994), 3.

10. Clement of Alexandria, *Stromata,* i., 305ff. See also Friedrich Max Muller, *The Six Systems of Indian Philosophy* (New York: Longmans, Green, and Co., 1899), 36.

11. John S. Dunne, *The Way of All the Earth* (South Bend, IN: Notre Dame Press, 1978), 44.

12. St. John of the Cross, *John of the Cross: Selected Writings,* ed. with an introduction by Kieran Kavanaugh, OCD (New York: Paulist Press, 1987), 91.

13. Frances G. Wickes, "The Inner World of Choice," *The American Scholar* 34 (January 1, 1965): 506.

CHAPTER TWO

1. Abraham H. Maslow, *The Farther Reaches of Human Nature* (Richmond, CA: Maurice Bassett, 1972), 344.

2. Richard McBrien, *Catholicism: New Study Edition* (San Francisco: HarperOne, 1994), 39.

3. Matthew Fox, *Meditations with Meister Eckhart* (New York: 1983), 30.

4. Emily Dickinson, "To This World She Returned," in *The Complete Poems of Emily Dickinson* (Boston: Little, Brown and Company, 1976), 402.

5. Huston Smith, "The Ambiguity of Matter," *Cross Currents* 48, no. 1 (Spring 1998).

6. Pierre Teilhard de Chardin, "Patient Trust," in Michael Harter, *Hearts on Fire: Praying with the Jesuits* (Chicago: Loyola Press, 2005), 102–3.

7. Nathanial Hawthorne, "Fancy's Show-Box," in *Twice-told Tales* (CreateSpace Independent Publishing Platform, 2013), 194.

8. Robert N. Bellah et al., *The Good Society* (New York: Vintage, 1992), 6.

9. Avery Dulles, *Models of the Church* (New York: Doubleday, 2002), 27.

10. Thich Nhat Hanh, *Vietnam: Lotus in a Sea of Fire* (New York: Hill and Wang, 1967), 94.

11. Ezra Pound, "An Object," 1912.

12. Edward Schillebeeckx, *Church: The Human Story of God*, vol. 10 of *The Collected Works of Edward Schillebeeckx* (London: Bloomsbury T&T Clark, 2014), 196.

13. Bellah, *Good Society*, 217.

14. Marcus J. Borg and John Dominic Crossan, *The First Paul: Reclaiming the Radical Visionary behind the Church's Conservative Icon* (San Francisco: Harper One, 2010), 205.

CHAPTER THREE

1. Mircea Eliade, *Myth and Reality* (Long Grove, IL: Waveland Press, 1998), 201.

2. Paul Tillich, *The Shaking of the Foundations* (Portland, OR: Wipf and Stock, 2012), 106.

3. C. G. Jung, *Memories, Dreams, Reflections*, rev. ed., recorded and ed. Aniela Jaffé, trans. Richard and Clara Williams (New York: Vintage Books, 1989), 340.

4. Teresa of Avila, *The Life of Saint Teresa of Avila by Herself*, trans. J. M. Cohen (New York: Penguin Classics, 1988), 55ff.

5. John Keats, *Autobiography of John Keats: Compiled*

from His Letters and Essays (Redwood City, CA: Stanford University Press, 1933), 253.

6. Ovid, *Fasti VI,* http://www.theoi.com/Text/Ovid Fasti6.html.

7. Cf. Joel Ryce-Menuhin, *Jung and the Monotheisms: Judaism, Christianity, and Islam* (Oxford, UK: Psychology Press, 1994), 101.

8. Bruce Sanguin, *Darwin, Divinity, and the Dance of the Cosmos* (Kelowna, BC: CopperHouse, 2007).

9. Matthew Arnold, "Emerson," *The Eclectic Magazine of Foreign Literature, Science, and Art* 103 (July–December 1884): 116.

10. *Lacrimae rerum* is the Latin phrase for "tears of things." It derives from bk. 1, line 462 of the *Aeneid* (c. 29–19 BCE) written by the Roman poet Virgil (Publius Vergilius Maro) (70–19 BCE).

11. William Shakespeare, *Hamlet,* act 3, scene 2.

12. Bernie S. Siegel, *Love, Medicine and Miracles: Lessons Learned about Self-Healing from a Surgeon's Experience with Exceptional Patients* (New York: William Morrow Paperbacks, 1998).

CHAPTER FOUR

1. Bernard J. Lee, ed., *Alternative Futures for Worship: The Eucharist* (Collegeville, MN: Liturgical Press, 1987), 31.

2. David Steindl-Rast, *Gratefulness, the Heart of Prayer: An Approach to Life in Fullness* (New York: Paulist Press, 1984), 39.

3. John Milton, *Paradise Lost,* book 6.

4. Edward Schillebeeckx, *Church: The Human Story of God* (New York: Crossroad Publishing Company, 1990).

5. William Shakespeare, *Troilus and Cressida,* act 4, scene 2.

6. C. G. Jung, *The Red Book: A Reader's Edition* (New York: W. W. Norton & Company, 2012), 128.

7. Ewert Cousins, *Bonaventure: The Soul's Journey into God* (New York: Paulist Press, 1978), 115.

8. Teilhard de Chardin, *Hymn of the Universe* (New York: HarperCollins, 1969), 13ff. See also the appendix, which provides a eucharistic prayer based on this quotation.

9. Pierre Teilhard de Chardin, "My Litany" (written on a picture of the Sacred Heart and found after his death).

10. See also David Richo, *The Sacred Heart of the World: Restoring Mystical Devotion to Our Spiritual Life* (New York: Paulist Press, 2007).

11. Karl Rahner, "The Theology of the Symbol," in *Theological Investigations,* vol. 4 (Baltimore: Helicon Press, 1966), 221–52.

12. Anselm of Canterbury, "Prayer to St. Mary (3)," in *The Prayers and Meditations of St. Anslem,* trans. Benedicta Ward (New York: Penguin Books, 1973), 121.

13. Paul Tillich, *Systematic Theology,* vol. 3 (Chicago: University of Chicago Press, 1963), 293–94.

14. Thomas Merton, "To the Immaculate Virgin, on a Winter Night," written in 1949, taken from the *National Catholic Reporter,* December 18, 1968.

CHAPTER FIVE

1. J. Dominic Crossan, *The Historical Jesus* (San Francisco: HarperOne, 1993), 344.

2. Idries Shah, *The Way of the Sufi* (London: Octagon Press, 2008), 165.

3. John Dear, "My Statement before the Judge," August 14, 2007, http://www.fatherjohndear.org/NCR_Articles/Jan22_08.html.

4. John Henry Newman, *An Essay in Aid of a Grammar of Assent* (London: Forgotten Books, 2010), 36ff.

5. Joseph Martos, *Doors to the Sacred: A Historical Introduction to the Sacraments in the Catholic Church* (St. Louis: Liguori Publications, 2014).

6. M. K. Gandhi, *My Non-Violence*, compiled by Sailesh Kumar Bandopadhyaya (Ahmedabad: Navajivan Publishing House), 20.

7. See Aelred of Rievaulx, "Dissertation on 'Earthly Paradise of Friendship.'" See also Robert Barzan, *Sex and Spirit* (San Francisco: White Crane Press, 1995), 27.

EPILOGUE

1. Cited by Avery Dulles, "The Ignatian Experience in the Theology of Karl Rahner," *Philippine Studies* 1, no. 3 (Manila: Ateneo de Manila University, 1965): 471–91. Originally from Karl Rahner, "Ueber die Erfahrung der Gnade" in *Schriften* 3.

2. Raimondo Panikkar, *Christophany* (Maryknoll, NY: Orbis, 2004), 146.

Other Paulist Titles by the Author

How to Be an Adult: A Handbook on Psychological and Spiritual Integration (1991) explores how we can evolve from the neurotic ego through a healthy ego to the spiritual Self so that we can deal with fear, anger, and guilt. It offers ways that we can be assertive, have boundaries, and build intimacy.

How to Be an Adult in Faith and Spirituality (2011) explores and compares religion and spirituality with an emphasis on how they can both become rich resources for personal growth. We increase our understanding of God, faith, and life's plaguing questions in the light of mysticism, depth psychology, and our new appreciation of evolutionary cosmology.

How to Be an Adult in Faith and Spirituality, CD (2012). This set of four CDs is compiled from a workshop given at Spirit Rock Retreat Center in California on how to design and practice an adult spirituality. They examine the spiritual riches in religion and how to discern what is not in keeping with our adult evolution.

The Sacred Heart of the World: Restoring Mystical Devotion to Our Spiritual Life (2007) explores the symbolism of the heart in world religious traditions, and then traces the historical thread of Christian devotion to the Sacred Heart of Jesus into modern times. The book focuses on the philosophy and theology of Teilhard de Chardin and Karl Rahner to design a new sense of what devotion can be.

When Love Meets Fear: How to Become Defense-less and Resource-full (1997). Our lively energy is inhibited by fear, and we are so often needlessly on the defensive. This book considers the origins and healings of our fears of closeness, commitment, aloneness, assertiveness, and panic attacks, so that we can free ourselves from the grip of fear that stops or drives us.

Other Titles by the Author

Being True to Life: Poetic Paths to Personal Growth. Boston: Shambhala, 2009.

Coming Home to Who You Are: Discovering Your Natural Capacity for Love, Integrity, and Compassion. Boston: Shambhala, 2012.

Daring to Trust: Opening Ourselves to Real Love and Intimacy. Boston: Shambhala, 2010.

The Five Things We Cannot Change and the Happiness We Find by Embracing Them. Boston: Shambhala, 2005.

How to Be an Adult in Love: Letting Love in Safely and Showing it Recklessly. Boston: Shambhala, 2013.

How To Be An Adult in Relationships: The Five Keys to Mindful Loving. Boston: Shambhala, 2002.

Mary within Us: A Jungian Contemplation of Her Titles and Powers. Berkeley, CA: Human Development Books, 2007.

The Power of Coincidence: How Life Shows Us What We Need to Know. Boston: Shambhala, 2007.

The Power of Grace: Recognizing Unexpected Gifts on the Path. Boston: Shambhala, 2014.

Shadow Dance: Liberating the Power and Creativity of Your Dark Side. Boston: Shambhala, 1999.

When the Past Is Present: Healing the Emotional Wounds That Sabotage Our Relationships. Boston: Shambhala, 2008.

Wisdom's Way: Quotations for Meditation. Berkeley, CA: Human Development Books, 2008.